W9-ADB-271

To the Young Writer

To the Young Writer

Hopwood Lectures, Second Series

EDITED BY A. L. BADER

ANN ARBOR PAPERBACKS

THE UNIVERSITY OF MICHIGAN PRESS

First edition as an Ann Arbor Paperback 1965
Copyright © by The University of Michigan 1965
All rights reserved
Library of Congress Catalog Card No. 65-14374
Published in the United States of America by
The University of Michigan Press and simultaneously
in Toronto, Canada, by Ambassador Books Limited
Manufactured in the United States of America

Acknowledgment is made for kind permission to quote the following copyrighted material.

"My Papa's Waltz" by Theodore Roethke. Copyright "My Papa's Waltz" 1942 by Hearst Magazines, Inc. from *Words for the Wind* by Theodore Roethke. Reprinted by permission of Beatrice Roethke.

Excerpts from *The Cantos of Ezra Pound*. Copyright 1934, 1948 by Ezra Pound. Reprinted by permission of the publishers, New Directions, and Arthur V. Moore.

"The Fury of Aerial Bombardment" from *Collected Poems 1930-1960* by Richard Eberhart. Copyright © Richard Eberhart 1960. Reprinted by permission of Oxford University Press, Inc. and Chatto and Windus Ltd.

"Before Disaster" from *Collected Poems* by Yvor Winters. Copyright 1952 by Yvor Winters. Reprinted by permission of New Directions.

"The Span of Life" from *Complete Poems of Robert Frost*. Copyright 1936 by Robert Frost. Copyright © 1964 by Lesley Frost Ballantine. Reprinted by permission of Holt, Rinehart and Winston, Inc. and Laurence Pollinger Ltd.

Selections from *Collected Poems 1923–1953* by Louise Bogan. Reprinted by permission of the publishers, Farrar, Straus and Giroux, Inc. Copyright 1929, 1935, 1937, 1941, 1954, 1963, 1964 by Louise Bogan. "Roman Fountain" and "To My Brother" were originally published in *The New Yorker Magazine*.

"His Confidence" from *The Winding Stair* by W. B. Yeats. Reprinted by permission of The Macmillan Company and A. P. Watt and Son (agent).

"His Confidence" from *Collected Poems of W. B. Yeats*. Reprinted by permission of Mrs. W. B. Yeats and Messrs. Macmillan & Co. Ltd.

FOREWORD

The Avery Hopwood and Jule Hopwood Awards in creative writing were established at The University of Michigan in 1930 in accordance with the terms of the will of the dramatist Avery Hopwood (class of 1905). Each year, at the time of the presentation of the awards, a lecture is given by a distinguished writer. The first collection of these lectures (1932–52) was published in 1954. The present volume consists of the twelve lectures delivered from 1953 through 1964.

As in the earlier collection, the lectures vary in subject matter. Some of the speakers concern themselves with technique, others with literary genres, with the criticism of individual writers, or with problems of the writer's training, of his gaining recognition, of his attitudes toward experience. Yet despite much variety of subject and diversity of critical opinion, all the speakers have in common an interest in the young writer and a desire to be useful to him.

FOREWORD

CONTENTS

THE YOUNG WRITER, PRESENT, PAST, AND FUTURE

by Stephen Spender

On this, the occasion of giving the annual Hopwood Awards, a few of you must be thinking about the first step in your career signified by receiving an award. In a rather varied life, one of the things I have never done is to win a literary prize. My first duty is to congratulate you on an achievement that fills me with admiration. But I must add a word of warning, which you can attribute to sour grapes if you wish. You only have to look at lists of Nobel Prizes, Pulitzer Prizes, and the rest to realize how changeable—if not fallible—is the judgment of literary juries.

In a way of course, this is rather consoling. To those of us—who are always in a democratic majority—who have not won prizes, it shows that we may be better than you who have. There is even more solid consolation to be derived from reflecting that those of us who do not deserve prizes may well win them, since the example of many who have won them shows that in the past there has not always been an absolutely necessary connection between prize-winning and desert.

Now that I'm on this aspect of the literary career—of which you are today tasting the first fruits—I may as well tell you that, economically speaking, being a writer is very like being a gambler. The story or article that earns you $10 might equally well earn you $1,000. Sometimes you are paid a few pennies for a review, sometimes enough to keep you for a month. And what is true of the economics of the thing is also true of reputation. Many writers living today who have great reputations

1

were hardly known during the long years when they were doing their best work. Anyone who has lived as a writer for twenty years or more knows too that one's stock goes up and down in what is a fluctuating market of critical opinions.

I mention these things in order to get them out of the way. The point really is that, although writers have to get started in one way or another with earning money and getting work published, these things are irrelevant. When I say irrelevant, I don't mean just that they don't matter; I mean that part of the struggle of being a writer is to watch and to be on guard that they don't have relevance. To be a failure can be discouraging. To be a success may mean something much worse: that you feel surrounded by people who want you to go on being one. Your publisher has sold fifty thousand copies of your last book, and is appalled when you bring in a manuscript of what may be a better book, but of which he knows he can sell only two thousand copies. The more you are known the more you discover that you are in some mysterious way arousing expectations in all sorts of individuals and groups of people who, since they read your work, feel that you have a certain responsibility towards them.

Shortly before he died, the English novelist, Sir Hugh Walpole, outlined to me the idea of a novel he wanted to write. It was on a subject very close to his heart, which he felt he understood better than others. From the way he spoke it was clear that this unwritten book was the one work in which he could portray his realest experience of life. However, it would describe people and behavior very different from those expected by the readers of his best-selling novels. I became excited at his idea and pressed him to start writing this book which I felt sure would be his masterpiece. "No," he said, "I shall never write it." "Why not?" "Because I could not write it in a way which would please my best-selling public. It would have to be produced in a small edition, for not more than two thousand readers. And after selling one hundred thousand copies of each of my novels, I could not endure that."

We can assume, I think, that anyone who simply wants to sell a lot of copies of his books will—if he knows this already—plan his career accordingly. He will not be a writer, but a businessman who is dealing with words as other people deal with any other mass-produced commodity. He will have no illusions, so he will not suffer at the end of his life from the kind of heartbreak which makes Sir Hugh Walpole— if a failure in his own art—the subject of a great biography by Rupert Hart-Davis, which has recently been published.

Now that the decks have been cleared of success and failure, what are the legitimate needs of the young writer? It's better, I think, to put the question in a form in which it can be examined by examples. What did the young writer of the past need, as the pre-conditions necessary to his gift?

Let us consider for instance, John Keats and Ernest Hemingway, two young men; one in London at the beginning of the nineteenth and the other in Paris at the beginning of this century.

What of Keats? Well, first of all, he wanted to write poetry for no reason except that he wanted to write poetry. His concept of poetry was formed from reading Spenser, Shakespeare, and, later, Milton. To him, poetry was the means of entering the world of other poets and then creating his own poems. Besides being a poet, he was a medical student, he was devoted to his brother Tom (whom he nursed through the consumption that he himself was very soon to die of), to his sister, Fanny Keats, and in the last months of his life, to Fanny Brawne, with whom he fell so hopelessly in love.

Poetry was for him a separate world from the real world of his medical studies, his brothers and sisters, even his love. Thus, in one of his letters he describes an occasion when the classroom or laboratory where he was studying suddenly disappeared, and he found himself in another world, even more real to him, of Shakespeare's *A Midsummer Night's Dream*. In another letter, written when he was nursing his brother, he complains that the identity of Tom Keats presses on him unendurably, a pressure he resents not out of selfishness but because he felt responsible to his world of poetry more even than to his brother. There was also something about his love for Fanny which seemed to him the surrender of his poetic world to a human one.

The next thing we note about the young Keats is that he wanted convivial friends who shared his love of poetry, provided that they did not press on him too much with their personalities. When he was twenty or so, he allowed himself to think that with Reynolds, Benjamin Robert Haydon, Cowden Clarke, Leigh Hunt and the rest, he had found a circle of enlightened people who recognized the same poetic values as he did. He wanted to belong to a group of friends who correspond very much to the group of French writers who will frequent the same Parisian cafe. Perhaps, in America today, this function of literary companionship is being fulfilled rather self-consciously, and with not enough frivolity to accompany the seriousness, by the creative writing courses. Brandy and coffee ought to be compulsory at all the creative writing seminars.

The next thing Keats wanted was to chart his course among the currents of literature and thought in his time. He disliked Pope's poetry, which he regarded as mere versification. He had very clearly developed ideas of his own about the world of pure imagination which poetry should create. He found precedents for his concept of poetry in Shakespeare. He was critical, though admiring, of Wordsworth. He was a not very generous rival of Shelley. He came to sneer at Leigh Hunt, and he grew out of the circle of his Hampstead friends into the isolation of genius.

Although he wrote that he had never allowed a shadow of public thought to enter his work, Keats was not without opinions. He was what we would call a liberal. He loved freedom (by which he meant Liberal Freedom) and hated Napoleon and the British government of his day.

Now let us turn to the young Hemingway in Paris a hundred years later. His attitudes are less literary than those of

Keats. He would deny, I think, having read much of anything, though he would admit to a great admiration for Stendhal. But don't let us be put off by his anti-literary pose without examining it more closely. He is not bookish, but he cares immensely about writing well, and takes a conscious pride in his use of words. Despite his pride, he goes humbly to Gertrude Stein and learns all he can from her about adding word to word with as much thought as if one were making a mosaic, and each word a separate stone.

Thus, the difference between the literary conscience of Hemingway and that of Keats may be the difference between romantic poet and modern novelist rather than that between man of literature and hairy-chested philistine. Hemingway knows that the roots of the novel are not in literature but in life. Although he can learn how to make sentences from Miss Stein and how to write about a battle from the description of Fabrice on the battlefield of Waterloo with which *The Charterhouse of Parma* opens—he sees that beyond learning how to write his own novels from other writers such a novelist must avoid literature like the plague. His source-books are the conversations of soldiers and drunks, the lonely thoughts of fishermen and hunters.

Just as much as Keats, Hemingway had then his special vision of a world of his imagination, a world in which love and drinks and fights and scenery were more real than, say, intellectual conversation, journalism, money, and stuffed shirts. In a drawing room his picture of prize fights, hunting in Africa, and war in Spain would doubtless drive out the china and chippendale, just as much as the world of *A Midsummer Night's Dream* came dancing down on a beam of sunlight into the room where Keats was learning medicine and made him forget the lecture.

Given the fact that he was trying to make novels out of life and not out of other novels, Hemingway also had his circle. Just as Keats, without very much success, looked in Hampstead for friends who shared his passion for the arts, Hemingway was looking for people who shared his passion for the real—which was the quality he wanted to put into his novels. They turned out to be bull-fighters, soldiers at Caporetto and in the front line at Madrid, and Americans in Paris. But the real Hemingway no more belongs to his tough circle than Keats to his Hampstead literati. The ultimate image we have of Hemingway is of the old man left fighting the fish of his art alone.

This is, indeed always, the situation of the artist with his vocation, pursuing his vision. All the same, he probably needs to start off from the fertilizing group of his friends who—perhaps only because they are generous and young, and do not themselves know as yet what they really want—form a magic circle round his youth.

Hemingway, like Keats, fought his battle among the ideas of his time. When he was lion-hunting in Africa he was also carrying on a polemic against Aldous Huxley, who had reproached him with being anti-intellectual. He showed pretty well, I think, that the intellect is a matter of passion and not of books. A few asides on his work about Goya and El Greco are impressive enough to make the reader realize that a writer with an understanding of painting does not need to show it all the time. Then, just as Keats without ever being what is called "political" wrote his sonnet to salute Leigh Hunt when he had been imprisoned for defamation by the British Government of that time, Hemingway took up the attitudes of an unpolitical man who loved freedom to the politics of the 1930's. *For Whom the Bell Tolls* corresponds in his work to Keats's sonnet celebrating Leigh Hunt when he was sent to prison. And all through his work there is a preoccupation with the relationship of those characters who are felt to be real because they have done real things—or because they have lived close to the values of nature—with the unreality of the politicians who direct the soldiers, the businessmen who have more power than the artists and the fishermen. For him freedom is the struggle of real life to assert itself against meddling and self-interested authority.

I could go on multiplying examples to illustrate that the young writer is someone with a mysterious sense of his own vocation, and a vision of reality which he wishes to communicate: to show, too, that in his youth he can benefit by the magic circle of those who are touched to sympathy by him, perhaps more for what he is than for what he does. His friends believe in *him* and they take his work on trust. Later on they become interested in other things—they cannot share his vocation—and he learns to be alone. But his youth has been watered by their sympathy.

He must certainly care for his craft as a writer. He must choose other writers who are guardian angels from the past whose works seem to be fighting on the side of his unborn poems or novels. What I very much doubt, though, is whether he should know more than this. One of the things that many modern writers perhaps suffer from is intellectual indigestion. We are told that Shakespeare had small Latin and less Greek, and the number of works he is supposed by scholars to have read would certainly not have filled even a small library. What he knew is so perfectly absorbed within his own genius that we are scarcely aware of his knowing it.

Shakespeare probably understood just so much of what he read as he required for the purpose of his writing. This is all a writer needs and it may be very little or it may be a great deal. With Dante and Milton it was a lot. A writer should think of every experience (and this includes the books he reads and the paintings he sees) in terms of the life which he is going to put into his work. He should be as much on guard against the corruption which comes from excessive sophistication and a too great load of learning as he is against any debasement of his gifts. Rimbaud advised writers to throw away dictionaries and reinvent words, and Blake thought that the forms in which past poets wrote became the shackles of new poetry. D. H. Lawrence, who was probably the most profound critic of modern values in this century, was utterly opposed to all the intellectual tendencies of our time, read little of his esteemed contemporaries, and not very selectively from the past.

None of these writers was an ignoramus, but all saw the necessity of approaching knowledge and theories about literature with the same lively precaution as you would enter a forest full of poison ivy and snares. They saw that intellectual life is not a passive process like hypnosis which you submit to, hoping that you will be entranced into doing something beyond your natural powers. You have to meet the intellectual work of others with your own powers, according to your capacity to cope with it, and not be overpowered by it. Intellectual life for a writer should be a struggle of all the forces of his life with other minds which he can meet on equal terms.

So here we have that timeless creature, the young writer, with his vocation, his vision of what is real to him, his magic circle of friends, the struggle of his whole existence within the ideas, the movements and the history of his time. He is timeless, and yet he is a kind of animal who tries to find the place within his time where he can best fulfill his gifts. He struggles to be received into the court of Queen Elizabeth or Louis XIV, or to be patronized by some great aristocrat of the eighteenth century, or to achieve the independence of a bourgeois living and working for himself in the nineteenth. He is a parasite, and often rather an ungrateful one. In her novel *Orlando,* Virginia Woolf describes the poet who comes to stay at Orlando's residence, where he charms everyone, and then goes away to write a perfidious lampoon on Orlando and his friends. When he claims his right to middle-class independence, as poets did in the nineteenth century, it is in order to spit on the bourgeois. He arrives as Rimbaud arrived in Paris in 1870, puts his feet up on the table of Madame Verlaine's clean dining room, takes out his pipe, smoking it upside down so that the hot ash falls onto her tablecloth, and shoos away her lap-dog, with the expletive comment: "Les chiens sont les liberaux."

But the position of the young writer differs according to the time in which he lives. His impossible behavior takes different forms according to whether he emerges from the cocoon of his family in 1450, 1550, 1650, 1750, 1850, or 1950, or whatever day of whatever year between these dates. In 1800 he is a revolutionary patriot, wild-eyed, unshaven, and influenced by the self-dramatizing self-pity and passion for freedom of Byron's *Prisoner of Chillon*. In 1900 he holds a lily in his hand, is languid, tired, dissipated, and infinitely superior to the universe. In 1914 he marches onto the battlefields of Europe and with a song on his lips proclaims that the world is about to be purified of ignoble qualities. In 1916 he is the voice of the youthful dead of both sides which hold no hatred for one another. By 1920 he has taken to alcohol and various other excesses, and he represents the naked, almost brutal assertion of his survival against a background of recently past death. He swears that whatever else happens, he will never be responsible towards anyone or anything again and he spits into the faces of the older generation. Under all these attitudes, he maintains the sense of his vocation. What in our time can the writer do, is the question he is asking, but by "doing" he means, how can he write his novels or poems. The answers are always changing, and as the time-process of our civilization speeds up they change from year to year with ever-increasing rapidity.

So the differences are less confusing when we recollect that the writer adopts attitudes for the sake of his writing. An attitude—or, for that matter, a literary movement—is the simplified statement of the relationship to his time which he adopts in order that he may best write his best work. Thus the young writers at the beginning of the French Revolution had to relate themselves to two things in contemporary history, which became one thing within their work. One was the changed attitude towards values which had been brought about by the French Revolution, the other was the fact that their immediate predecessors were writing in a style which could not possibly be the vehicle for the altered sensibility resulting from the change from aristocratic values to democratic ones. These two things became one imaginative life within the colloquial manner of writing of Wordsworth, the romanticism of Keats.

What is the writer's vision, though? With the poet it is his significant experience expressed in a poetic idiom which responds or is sensitive to the circumstances of his time. The poet's ideas of what is most valuable, because most living is experience, confront the world with his idiom of the contemporary human situation. The novelist illustrates, in his depiction of character, the struggle of individual human existence within the circumstances of a particular historic period. The young man Tolstoi shows us a whole panorama of the circumstances of individuals living through the Napoleonic wars. Although *War and Peace* is all, in a sense, a depiction of life, the values of living are only realized at their most intense in moments of the lives of particular characters. Moments of Natasha's vivid childhood, of Pierre Bezukhov's changes of heart—most of all perhaps the moment when Prince Andrew lies wounded on the battlefield. The novel portrays the struggle for the realization of life within the circumstances of living. If the conditioning circumstances are not truly imagined and portrayed within the work, then the life in the novel seems false; and if the circumstances are realized, then the work becomes a depressing exercise in what is called realism.

There is no way in which a writer can cheat himself into having a greater awareness of life than his genius has given him. There are, however, circumstances and conditions which can cheat him out of the possibility of realizing his gifts. It is more difficult to be a young writer at some periods than at others. There are some decades when the mood of the time seems to permit of a much wider realization of the values of living than others. In England the Elizabethan age was certainly such a time. There are others when a great many writers work under circumstances where life itself seems weighed down and oppressed, and yet the material development of society is so expansive and confident that masterpieces are written. The Victorian Age was such a period. But although nineteenth-century England was ebullient and expansive, yet it is really the literature of France in this period which tells us more of what was happening to the spirit of man.

"What is the position of the young writer today?" That is the question at the back of my mind all the time that I have been talking. For it seems to me that in certain ways this question is more difficult to answer than it has been for a great many years.

The reason it is difficult to answer is that the one thing that previously was clear about the position of the writer has suddenly become amorphous. What has been clear for so long was his extreme individuality. The writer has for a hundred and fifty years regarded himself and been regarded as an independent creator or critic within society who brought to it his own vision or who attacked it from the point of view of a detached observer. For instance, we think of Keats and the other romantics as being outside the materialism of the industrial revolution. Perhaps they opposed the materialism of the nineteenth century, or perhaps they added something to life which made circumstances tolerable and even justified modern civilization. Whichever it was they did, rightly or wrongly, we think of them as *outside* their society. The French poets, like Baudelaire, Verlaine, and Rimbaud, we think of as still more savagely isolated individualists, who were antagonistic to all contemporary values. We think, too, of the novelists either as being critics of Victorianism who judged their age from a disinterested point of view or as truthful observers of character, who were able to indicate the points at which life acquires the greatest significance. Flaubert's *The Sentimental Education*, for example, is a scrupulous and exact study of the lives of a group of individuals against a background of history, and at the end we are able to measure the extent to which Frederic Moreau and the other characters have lived their lives, attained happiness, suffered to some purpose, created beauty, or loved.

Today we suddenly find ourselves living in a world where it is very difficult to think of the poet creating a unique vision like that of Keats, which will so enormously enhance the value of living for his readers that his poetry will seem a system of the imagination where "beauty is truth, truth beauty," and nothing else need be added to life. It is equally difficult to think of the novelist being an independent, detached critic of society. We suddenly find that the individual visions, which right up to the time of the aesthetic movement could add something so significant within art to the value of life that ordinary life itself seemed scarcely worth living, have shrunk into private fantasies, childhood memories, squibs like Truman Capote's novel about some people who decide to go and live in a tree—or like Henry Miller's books in which all his characters indulge themselves to the utmost in physical sensation and have no philosophy or, purpose beyond such indulgence.

What has happened is that the idea that there are writers and other artists and sensitive individuals who in some way can preserve an integrity and create beauty outside the materialism of society, has suddenly been completely shattered. We may not live in a totalitarian world, but a kind of totalitarianization of the spirit has overtaken all of us. In a world where within a matter of hours or days the whole of our civilization may be destroyed, or where if this does not happen we may find our minds the passive objects of political dictatorship, using psychological propaganda, everyone shares with everyone else such enormous secrets of fear and anxiety that the idea of being outside what is happening—as Keats in his way, and Dickens in his quite different way, were outside it—seems impossible. Indeed a writer, like T. S. Eliot, who does retain a certain outsideness, only manages to do so by describing a religious experience which is outside time and history altogether.

We cannot imagine that the young writer of genius will today believe himself to be a unique person in a unique position bringing to other people a picture of living values which will change the lives of those who have eyes to see and ears to hear. Instead now of an art which will add another world of the imagination to the material world, we have literature of young novelists which, however eccentric or fantastic it may seem, is really documentary. Someone who lives in the deep South had some very extraordinary and crazy relatives whom he is going to tell us about. Someone else had a very odd relationship with one of the masters at his preparatory school or at the military academy. A woman who was frustrated in her desire to become cultured never got to the Museum of Modern Art, so she became a nymphomaniac, upset her family badly and was finally taken away in a van. All these experiences can be original and it is possible to write about them well, but they do not enhance the life of the reader, and they do not criticize the world in which we are living. No amount of odd experience and good writing and all the characters going mad can really get away from the fact that they are really just embroidered documentary material.

In these circumstances, the young writer is tempted to abandon his artistic responsibility—that is, his responsibility to do what he knows he alone can do in the way he alone can do it. On every side, there are voices which say: "Don't be responsible to yourself. It is no longer any use. Be responsible to us." In England he is invited to become an agent for disseminating culture through the British Broadcasting Corporation, or the British Council. In the United States he is invited to join a university to become a teacher of creative writing, with a certain real though vaguely defined responsibility to the academic world. Meanwhile a tremendous critical apparatus based on a study of the past works of writers, most of whom hated the very idea of critics and criticism, grows up, and rules about technique, influences, myths, and so on are extracted from past works, which get very near to supplying the young with objective formulae for creating new ones. There is a great deal of talk about Freud and Jung and the unconscious, but the fact that writing should be a process of whose development the writer himself should be largely unconscious is forgotten. At this point it may be well to remind ourselves that Goethe observed to Eckermann that it would be impossible in the future for any poet to attain the stature of Shakespeare. The reason he gave for this conclusion was that the result of contemporary criticism would make it impossible for any poet to develop, as Shakespeare did, without being self-conscious about his own development. The true development of a poet like Shakespeare —Goethe thought—was like that of a man who walks in his sleep.

The temptation of the writer of yesterday—W. H. Auden has said—was to be too individualistic, too proud, too isolated. But the temptation of the writer today—he went on—is to prostitute himself, to make slight concessions all the way round: to the academies, to the cultural agencies, to the glossy magazines which have decided that they want to publish something "better" than they have done before, but not too good.

In the present situation it is extremely difficult to say what is the right course for the young writer. You can't, as you would perhaps do in the past, advise "Find the right patron who will give you the freedom to do your best work which will glorify his name," nor yet "Create in your work the vision of an inner life of aesthetic values which will enable your readers to escape the vulgarity and banality of modern living"; nor "Take sides with the cause which represents greater human freedom and draw strength from the life and future of the just cause you support." It is not as easy as that. Nor do I accept the despairing view of George Orwell in his very interesting essay on Henry Miller, entitled *Inside the Whale*. Orwell says in words which I paraphrase: "Accept the fact that you can do absolutely nothing to alter the condition of the world today. Make a virtue of necessity, and like Jonah, use your art to get inside the whale. Don't object, don't rebel, just accept everything and then make the best of the circumstances of a life of private sensations and experience which is still possible to you." His own book, *1984*, like Camus' novel, *The Plague*, refutes him. It is still possible, by trying to see the largest truth about the time in which we live, and by simply stating it, to get outside the whale.

Meanwhile, one can also say that there are certain things which are wrong, and even a few which are right. It may be necessary to accept the situation of working in a more official capacity—as a teacher, or a cultural agent—than before, but it is still not necessary to sell your soul. By selling your soul I mean not cherishing the distinction between work which one does to satisfy one's own standards and that done to satisfy other people's standards. One's own standards are simply to write about the truth as one experiences it, in the way in which one can write about it. To discover these two things is already the task of a lifetime, and by simply devoting oneself to them one may solve the problems which I have stated here.

Another positive thing which I can say is that the young should be an audience for one another. In this the creative writing courses, of which I feel critical in some ways, offer a tremendous opportunity to young writers. It may not be that all of you are going to be writers, but there is every reason why all of you should be interested in the writing of each one of you. The interest that you can give to the writer who is going to be outstanding among you is the equivalent, at this stage of his development, to a blood transfusion. And it is blood which only the young can give to others who are young, because later on in life everyone is too preoccupied with his own affairs to give so generously. No one ever receives in all his life any praise which is comparable to that which one receives when one has sent one's first work to a friend who feels it to be a new and exciting experience in his own life.

The most important thing of all, though, is to have an absolutely sacred sense of the vocation of being a writer. A writer is a person who experiences with part of himself the life around him and with some other part of himself the life of those past writers whose works have filled him with the desire to be a writer. In his own work he relates his sense of that past with his awareness of this present. In doing so he creates something entirely new, and this new thing, if it is worthy, is to write the words which the past master would write about contemporary life if he were now living. Through the contemporary writer's hand flows the blood of past writers, and to the degree that the present writers fulfill their vocation they are extending into the future the life of the old. There remains the problem of relating oneself to the present situation. But the true writer lives in a past and a future situation for which the present is only a bridge. This reduces the contemporary problem to its true proportions. It means that although you must be aware of the present situation you must see it in the light of the past and future, pursue your vocation, write as well as you can and not better than you can, provide an audience for your contemporaries, and judge life from the center of your artistic conscience, to which you are alone responsible.

MODERN PLAYWRITING AT THE CROSSROADS

by John Gassner

Thomas Carlyle is supposed to have replied to a eulogy on a starry sky that it was "a sair nicht"—a sorry night, indeed. And I have neither the genius nor the dyspepsia of Carlyle to warrant obscuring the luster of the present occasion. Yet sobering considerations are never amiss when the subject is the present-day theatre; and thoughts out of season are in season when the subject is playwriting. There is, besides, a certain comfort in the impulse to criticize the stage. To criticize it is to acknowledge an interest in its condition, and the theatre thrives on being noticed. Criticism is construed as a challenge, and the theatre likes to be challenged.

The theatre has been in a crisis for well over a decade, and in no respect has it been more disappointing than in the calibre of new plays. Like other contemporary writers, the playwright has been disoriented; but more than other writers, he has betrayed his disorientation because he works under extreme disadvantages. He must address a large public, which responds to his work very manifestly under the influence of the time spirit. He must also satisfy excessive requirements imposed, on the one hand, by the extravagant faith reposed in him—from sixty thousand to a hundred and twenty thousand dollars' worth of faith in the case of a Broadway production—and, on the other hand, by the extreme insecurity of theatrical production. Rarely, besides, does the playwright complete a final pre-production version without having followed extensive suggestions from his producer. Rarely does he rework his play during

17

the rehearsal and try-out periods without pressure from the stage director. Many of the author's afterthoughts, moreover, simply cannot be incorporated in the playing-text because it is too late for his actors to discard old lines and learn new ones. Rarely, in other words, does the playwright enjoy conditions that would allow him to straighten out his thinking and artistry if he has not already mastered his confusions and ambivalences. And, finally, his play receives keener scrutiny, as a rule, than the work of the director and the actors, so that disorientation on his part can become a major disaster. Since critics are themselves members of the writing profession, they are in a position to find chinks in the playwright's armor, if not indeed bats in his belfry.

His situation in our time, however, goes well beyond the normal hazards of his craft. It is the condition of dramatic art at the mid-century point that is most relevant to the playwright's problem, once we grant that playwriting is always difficult and talent always rare. It is an error to assume that an art remains stable; that it presents the same opportunities and challenges in one period that it does in another. In the theatre, instability is particularly marked, and the incidence of diminishing returns for certain kinds of substance and style is extraordinarily high. It is entirely possible, for example, that the Eugene O'Neill of 1920 or the Clifford Odets of 1935 would have had a lukewarm reception in 1950. It is important, therefore, to arrive at perspectives on the over-all condition of playwriting at this time.

Instinctively or occupationally, all effective writers are aware of this fact to some degree. Arthur Miller and Tennessee Williams, at the present time, have given serious thought to their problems as writers in an age of anxiety and failure, or as newcomers in the modern theatre, which by now has three-quarters of a century of trial and error behind it. As a rule, however, playwrights need to be made aware of the situation in their craft, because they tend to confuse a perspective with mere accommodation to fashion. The practical playwright is usually aware of current interests rather than of the broad stream of development in his art. And since the rise of realism in the nineteenth century, he has been peculiarly inclined to view his obligation as one of echoing popular interests. As a result, indeed, he succumbs to mediocrity to the degree that mediocrity is inherent in his subject. Alfred North Whitehead wrote that "Tennyson was a great poet with a mediocre subject"—namely, Victorian England. Playwrights often suffer the same fate. Those who write for the stage are surely more susceptible to the seductions of the moment than to a broad view of their situation.

I believe it is of the utmost importance for playwrights to realize that they are standing at the crossroads of modern drama. That is my first proposition! They are now called upon to choose one of two ways of writing for the stage—the way of the *reporter* and the way of the *creator*. And they must choose the latter if the stage is to survive the competition of the mass media, which has grown enormously and is likely to become even severer. Just as playwrights, especially in America, can no longer compete with routine farces and melodrama, now the stock in trade of the mass-communication media, so they can no longer compete against motion picture and television cameras with slices of life or facsimile reproductions of humdrum reality.

Nevertheless, the playwright hesitates at the crossroads. He does so, because the way of the reporter once proved satisfactory, or at least profitable, and was, moreover, equated with truthfulness and significance. At the same time, he is wary of flights into imaginative art because these have so often represented a retreat from reality, a rejection of popular theatre, or a sterile Bohemianism. More than he realizes, however, his preference for so-called down-to-earth reportorial drama is the result of misconceptions. In writing conventionally, he confuses the drama of stencils with the dramatic realism that gave the theatre its modernity and claim to importance after 1880.

He fails to realize that the masters of realistic drama were creators of life *in the drama* rather than sedulous imitators of life *outside the theatre.* The modern masters shaped an experience out of the substance of their passion and intellect, instead of setting up a camera in the streets or the family parlor and letting the camera click mechanically. The new playwright, especially in the American theatre, fails to distinguish sharply enough between an Ibsen or a Chekhov and any of the numerous mediocrities who have taken the name of realism in vain. Nor does he distinguish sufficiently between pseudo-poetic artificers and true poets of the theatre. He concludes from *avant-garde* aberrations by Cummings, Cocteau, or Gertrude Stein that these represent the only alternatives to his kind of still-life or, shall I say, "dead-life," realism. He takes the *ersatz* article of pseudo-modernism at the valuation placed upon it by its exponents; whereupon he concludes that there are no satisfactory alternatives to the debased realism which passes for currency in show-business.

Conversely, *anti-realists,* reacting to pseudo-realism, have drawn their own erroneous conclusions. Too many of them, upon observing the commonplace stage, conclude that it is high time to swing from a flying trapeze and thumb noses at the bourgeoisie as a reliable method of creating a new dramatic art. They assume that anything that contravenes realism is *ipso facto* art, thus mistaking ambiguity for profundity and sensationalism for creative potency.

The situation is by no means new, of course. It could be observed in many respects during previous decades. What *is* new is the severity of the situation in our times, for today the novelty has worn off from both realism and anti-realism as technical or stylistic principles of dramatic composition. The so-called realistic playwright can no longer count on making an impression because he has provided an accurate picture. Nor can any anti-realistic playwright startle playgoers into delight merely because he has drawn everything topsy-turvy. The sensationalism of realism and the sensationalism of anti-realism are by now equally passé.

Most important to the state of dramatic art, however, is not the fact that a playwright can no longer win success or esteem on factitious grounds of novelty, but the fact that certain factors that once gave impetus to his writing are no longer sufficiently operative.

I have in mind the need of some stimulus for writers who are obliged to affect a large congregated public. They must be energized by aims and challenges, or perceptions and ideals other than the mere ambition to write plays for the market place. For direct public presentation, which is the essence of theatre, writers need a sense of relatedness. They develop best as significant playwrights when convinced that they are not creating in a vacuum. And for a vaulting mind and spirit, even the theatre considered as an autonomous institution *is essentially a vacuum.* "Theatre for theatre's sake" may serve not only as a flattering slogan for showmen, but as a deterrent to strictly utilitarian expectations from the stage. It has also been necessary to *re-theatricalize* the modern stage, which had been too grimly *de-theatricalized* by doctrinaire naturalism. But "theatre for theatre's sake" has never been able to nourish memorable play-writing. It has never been a substitute for a ruling passion and relatedness; as John Livingston Lowes declared, "the imagination never operates in a vacuum." A sense of extra-theatrical purpose is as marked in the work of an effective anti-realist like Bertolt Brecht as in the work of a great realist like Ibsen, as decisive in the comic genius of a Bernard Shaw as in the tragic sense of an O'Neill or an O'Casey. These playwrights believed with Mussorgsky that "Art is not an end in itself, but a means of addressing humanity." And it is, in my opinion, to the weakening of extra-theatrical purpose, to the loss of creative incentives mere show-business cannot provide, that we must attribute at least some of the flatness of contemporary play-writing.

Adventurousness was a major stimulus after 1880 in all the major theatres of the West because opinion was mainly rebell-ion against one convention or another. And when rebellion was not an efficient cause, the spirit of criticism was. The modern drama was born in rebellion and cradled in criticism. Intelligence, vigor, and vivacity were attendant upon this modern adventure and were its dramatic and esthetic correlates. They were especially attendant upon this adventure in the case of dramatic realism. Along with personal qualities of style and personal qualities of mind, the spirit of inquiry provided the esthetic attributes of the work, whether the author's appraisals of his world were as direct as Ibsen's or as indirect as Chekhov's. One reason why pioneering modern realism was not flaccid, as most realistic plays have been since the nineteen-forties, is that it was critical realism.

The critical spirit led to adventurousness in dramatic art itself. Personal passion led to individual style rather than routinized prose. And the need for making a special view apparent led to the adoption of dramatic structure that carried realistic dramaturgy well beyond the mere adoption of the fourth-wall convention of pretending that actions transpire on the stage exactly as they do off-stage without an audience.

Citing only familiar examples, I would recall the highly individual style and form of Ibsen, Strindberg, Chekhov, Shaw, and O'Casey. To note the distinctiveness of the work we need only observe Ibsen's development of a retrospective, stock-taking, discussion-pyramided type of drama which first appeared in *A Doll's House* and culminated in *John Gabriel Borkman;* or Strindberg's intense concentration on crisis to the exclusion of other elements of plot in such plays as *The Father, Miss Julie, The Creditor,* and that gripping divorce-drama *The Link;* or Chekhov's contrapuntal and off-center, centrifugal weave of action; or Shaw's dialectical brilliance in melodrama, farce, and comedy of ideas; or O'Casey's lyrical pathos and mordancy. Nor did such distinctive realists lose a distinctive style when they chose to abandon the realistic technique. They were still bent upon having their say in their own manner when Ibsen adopted symbolism, when Strindberg turned to expressionism, or when Shaw wrote *Heartbreak House* as a "fantasia in the Russian manner," to cite his own subtitle.

Associated with critical realism were, of course, other factors than the adventure of opinion. One of these was the sheer

pleasure of intellectualism, most conspicuously in Shaw's writing; for intellect was once considered a distinction rather than a detriment, say I nostalgically! A playwright was expected to have a mind, and he gloried in its possession. Another factor was principle, or the belief that a playwright could not be modern unless he possessed integrity. He could not be modern if he moderated or vulgarized reality for the sake of approval—which explains the critic Shaw's contemptuous description of the pseudo-Ibsenist Pinero as a playwright who had no idea "beyond that of doing something daring and bringing down the house by running away from the consequences." Not surprisingly, then, the true modernist, in the theatre between 1880 and 1939, usually had his pioneering work produced by experimental stage groups. In Europe, moreover, such work was less taxed by the requirement of serving commercial enterprise because the play appeared in repertory, whereas nowadays, especially on Broadway, a play that does not win immediate success is quickly laid in lavender. If a play does not promise popular success in our high-cost theatre, the work is either tailored to suit the market or denied a professional stage production. Only recently, within the past two or three years, has there been a slight swing away from the commodity-philosophy of play production. Yet laudable as have been off-Broadway enterprises at a Circle-in-the-Square or a Theatre de Lys in New York, they are still no substitute for the repertory system. Nor are these groups sparked by that dedication to the development of a dramatic movement relevant alike to art and society which inspired the Théâtre Libre, the Abbey Theatre, the Art Theatre in Moscow, the Provincetown Players in New York.

A sense of discovery was also a powerful ferment of dramatic modernism, whether discovery took the form of naturalistic scientism and sociology, now properly outmoded, or psychological exploration, such as Strindberg and Wedekind undertook. Nor should we slight the efforts of playwrights to discover the common earth and the common man. The discovery of unfashionable life for the theatre gave us the plays of Synge and

O'Casey, Tolstoy's *The Power of Darkness* and Gorki's *The Lower Depths,* and the first plays of O'Neill and Odets—to mention familiar instances.

Finally, the playwrights were likely to benefit from the stimulus of visionary optimism. They had an active faith in man, however greatly scientific determinism tended to reduce man's tragic stature. Without that faith there would have been little point in Ibsen's or Shaw's prodding or haranguing him, or in exposing his frustrations in a particular society.

It may be argued that the pioneering playwrights were deluded; that they suffered from the fallacy and pathos of modern liberalism. It cannot be denied, however, that they derived purposefulness, passion, and even exuberance from their faith. Believers in progress may become the dupes, even the victims, of progress, but confidence and a sense of engagement are anything but deterrents to dramatic vigor. Can one doubt this conclusion after comparing the difference in voltage between Odets' early and late plays, or between the plays Shaw wrote before 1914 and those he wrote after 1930?

Today, playwriting is too rarely galvanized by many factors that once gave realism its incisiveness, resolve, and vitality. The Ibsenism of Arthur Miller proves that these qualities are not unattainable even today, and playwriting was somewhat energized in France, England, and America during the Second World War. But, in general, opinion has lacked fervor; and criticism, edge. Inquiry and exploration have been rare and affirmations few, in the contemporary theatre. We have had, in the main, a tepid, if not indeed pusillanimous, stage. Even the occasional scintillations of comedy have too often occurred in a vacuum. Character has been infrequently probed. Realism has been expended mainly upon surface-manifestations. Even negations, except in O'Neill's *The Iceman Cometh,* have been mild and circumspect.

That a disenchantment pervasive in our world should have affected playwrights is hardly surprising. It is understandable, too, that in view of the contemporary situation, playwrights are now wary of social prescriptions that had been popular in the theatre of the nineteen-thirties. One does not expect writers to *will* themselves into believing untenable postulates for man or society. But I see them as writers who are immobilized at the crossroads of modern theatre because they have not yet learned to make anything out of their *disbelief*.

Their disenchantment has no substantiality; it is mute, rather than expressive. Without trying to account for current apathy, I venture to describe their condition as intellectual sloth, as hesitancy to let the mind or spirit assert itself even in disenchantment. It may be that the alternative to the old critical realism sparked by optimism is a new critical realism sparked by disillusion. As yet, however, playwrights, especially in the American theatre, have shown little aptitude for this second kind of realism.

Since Western theatre is now eclectic, our playwrights can, of course, elect a non-realistic style of theatre, as an alternative. They can even elect dramatic estheticism without necessarily disintegrating the modern stage. The test, however, will be the same as for realism—namely, achievement.

Nihilism or disintegration, it is true, became pronounced in nonrealistic dramaturgy during and after the First World War. It became marked in the case of the expressionists, dadaists, and surrealists. Ranging from the cult of symbolism, which can be traced as far back as the 1890's, to the cult of frenzy that had a brief vogue on the European continent after 1914, anti-realism proved largely arid only at this latter end of the spectrum. Estheticism maintained at least a belief and an adventurousness in art, besides correcting the excesses of naturalism. Dedication to art is considerably more fruitful than the dedication to precisely nothing which characterizes the commercial stage in our time. An "art for art's sake" policy, if carried to logical conclusions, may be a sign of decadence, but estheticism has its own assertiveness, too. It demands integrity from the artist, requiring him to respect his sensibility and to attain a high degree of artistry in the service of style and form. The pursuit of art for art's sake has obvious limitations but can be in some respects affirmative and humanistic. The esthetic movement, too, left a legacy to playwrights of the present generation. That it can still be drawn upon is especially attested in our theatre by the estheticism of Tennessee Williams.

Moreover, there is no reason to assume that estheticism cannot draw upon the resources of modern realism even while discarding realistic dramaturgy and peephole stage conventions. The vital elements of realism remained in force, for example, when the late Jean Giraudoux wrote plays infused with critical intelligence. There is no essential conflict between the aims of modern realism and of poetic extravaganza in, let us say, *The Madwoman of Chaillot* any more than there was essential conflict between the realism of *Ghosts* and that of *Man and Superman*, including its *Don Juan in Hell* fantasy. The same intellectual strenuousness is present equally in Strindberg's late expressionist and early naturalistic dramas. Nor has there been anything but strenuous intellectualism in such anti-naturalist plays of Bertolt Brecht as *The Three-Penny Opera*, *Mother Courage*, and *The Good Woman of Setzuan*. There is no intrinsic incompatibility between adventurousness in the domain of opinion and adventurousness in the domain of art. If such incompatibility has often manifested itself, it has been occasioned by the ineptitude of would-be realists and the vacuousness of would-be esthetes.

If playwrights, especially in America, seem incapable of availing themselves of the possibilities inherent in modern nonrealistic art, the reason is twofold. On the one hand, faith in art as a sufficient goal in the theatre is at a low ebb, and has been that, indeed, ever since the social idealism of the thirties discredited an "art for art's sake" viewpoint. On the other hand, the infusion of nonrealistic dramaturgy with the critical spirit never made much headway in the American theatre after the twenties. Today, moreover, the critical spirit is so enervated that it does not invigorate nonrealistic drama any more than it invigorates realistic drama. Tennessee Williams' *Camino Real*, the most recent American experiment in the symbolist-expressionist style, was as embarrassingly callow in its thinking as in its literary effusiveness. If British poetic drama, as written by Eliot and Fry, cannot be charged with callowness, it is not exempt from another charge—that of sterility. I would make a grudging exception only in favor of *The Cocktail Party* and *The Lady's Not for Burning*. Strong claims have been made for the work of Jean Anouilh in France, but as yet I cannot validate them myself, and I doubt that posterity will. In no country's theatre, now that Giraudoux has been dead for a decade and Brecht is isolated behind the Iron Curtain like a chaffinch in a cage, can I discern any dramatic stylization distinguished by vitality.

Modern playwriting, then, is enfeebled today because neither the realistic nor the esthetic legacy retains its pristine potency. Both styles of modern theatre have suffered much deterioration from within—realism because it became too commonplace, estheticism because it became too empty and pretentious. The failings of each mode of modernism were inherent in the mode, as we can observe in assessing the dry texture of Ibsen's realistic plays and the vaporous quality of Maeterlinck's symbolist efforts. In many instances, their successors merely exaggerated the faults—latter-day realists increasing the commonplaceness, while latter-day anti-realists increased the vapor. The contemporary social and political situation plagues playwriting today, making it placid and evasive or superficial, but its deficiencies and defects have been intrinsic to modern dramatic art itself. Inherited tendencies exact their toll, and the past must share the blame for present failure. Bad example stalemated realism and discredited estheticism.

Specifically, we must observe this about the realistic mode of modern drama—that realistic writing became too largely the writing of problem plays, transforming the theatre into a reformatory; or became the writing of propaganda plays, converting the stage into a soap-box; or became the writing of nondescript pieces of description, turning theatrical art into a placid mirror in which the public could see itself making usually unimpressive faces. Today, neither subtlety nor wit, neither incisiveness nor profundity, neither originality nor any other sort of transcendence of the obvious characterizes all but a minute fraction of the once-impressive realistic theatre. During the Broadway season now coming to an end only two exceptions could be noted, *The Caine Mutiny* and *Tea and Sympathy,* and this has been considered an exceptionally good season. Moreover, the first-mentioned play was extracted from a novel.

Specifically, too, we may observe this about the nonrealistic modern theatre—that it has too often compounded confusion and whipped-up froth. Expressionism and surrealism discredited themselves with their excesses. Poetic drama has too often been *willed* into existence or academically pursued in the modern theatre, except when distilled from folklore in exotic regions. And folk-life has become a diminishing source of poetry on our contracting planet. Poetry as *tour de force* verse drama, gratifying in a few Christopher Fry plays, gives no evidence of a tuneful summer. Nor has formalism recommended itself as a modern style, so that its ablest recent proponent, T. S. Eliot, has himself increasingly abandoned it since the writing of *Murder in the Cathedral* in 1935; and the formalism of William Butler Yeats's fine latter-day plays, patterned after Japanese drama, amounted to an almost complete withdrawal from the public theatre. An esoteric drama for the élite has never before contributed greatly to a renascence of playwriting.

Estheticism, despite the noteworthy contributions of a Gordon Craig or Jacques Copeau to the theatre arts, did not give sufficient sustenance to playwriting, and is even less likely to do so at present. A success of theatrical art or so-called *coup de théâtre* by, let us say, the Habimah Theatre of Israel or the Jean-Louis Barrault Company of Paris is one thing; the creation of potent modern drama is another. The Old Vic or the Stratford Company, gifted in the art of stylization, may provide a glossy or even excellent production of Shakespeare, but does not give the modern stage another Shakespeare; not even another Ben Jonson, Ibsen, or Shaw. And in previous decades, a virtuoso director such as Meyerhold may have brought forth prodigious feats of staging without bringing forth a single prodigy of playwriting.

Standing between seedy realism and motley theatricalism, the contemporary playwright is likely to be cross-ventilated to no particular benefit to his art or his public; especially in the American professional theatre where the unstimulating realistic play usually expires on the boards and the stylized play rarely reaches them. Nodding in the direction of debased realism, an Elmer Rice has both an artistic and financial fiasco with *The Winner* or with an earlier problem play such as *A New Life*. And gazing in the opposite direction of turgid, symbolic estheticism, a Tennessee Williams bravely runs into a fog with a *Camino Real*.

Where then may the playwright, whose plight is not entirely alien to his colleagues in fiction and nondramatic poetry, take his stand? I cannot adopt a Pisgah view in order to direct the new playwright toward some Promised Land. But it may be neither impossible nor impertinent to direct his gaze toward possibilities suggested by past experience and present exigency. I would suggest therefore that the playwright consider the following possibilities of breaking his present impasse:

Let him pursue the way of realism, if he inclines in that direction; but let him reject photography. Let his *perception* and *apprehension* be realistic. Whether he adopts the method of direct assault upon reality or some indirect Chekhovian method, he is entirely free to avail himself of an imaginative presentation. Without such presentation, *The Glass Menagerie* would have been tenuous and the current season's *Teahouse of the August Moon* either pointless or inert. Without the modified expressionism Arthur Miller mingled with realism, *Death of a Salesman* would have been humdrum, especially in view of the representative commonplaceness of his Willy Loman.

A contemporary playwright's art does not have to be humdrum because his characters lack brilliance or some other unusual attribute. His imagination should be able to give them dimension and stature; he should not shy away from suffering and exultation but remember that only commonplace people dislike tragedy, because as Masefield said, "they dare not suffer and cannot exult." Moreover, imaginative form can transfigure subject matter. The *form* can be poetic. And, especially on stage, the playwright can bring into being a "poetry of the theatre" in the organization or sequence, shape, and high-lighting of the episodes of a play. Treadmill playwriting—that is, walking the treadmills of an ordinary time-sequence and routine exposition—is unnecessary. It can actually prove detrimental to the higher realism of exposing the truth.

Poetry can also be achieved in realistic drama by attention to nuance and to atmosphere and mood. Too many plays are written today without sensibility, too many without a dominant feeling or feeling-tone in individual scenes and in the play as a whole. Also, insufficient stress is placed on variety of scene within the unity of the play. Action is shown under a glare of white light, without any concern for chiaroscuro. Language, too, is susceptible to enrichment and intensification without violence to artistic, as opposed to phonographic, plausibility. Both colloquial and formal dialogue can be cadenced and ac-centuated; and it can be enriched with rhythm and imagery without our resorting to reminiscent patterns or literary echoes.

Realism does not need to be cravenly imitative in portrayal and description. It can even be discreetly symbolic and sugges-tive, as such veteran realists as Ibsen and Chekhov teach us in, let us say, *The Wild Duck, The Sea Gull,* and *The Cherry Orchard.* Nor do ideas have to be argued with a "massive retalia-tion" technique. They can be parceled out and orchestrated, or counterpointed.

The play of ideas should *play* rather than bombard. It is conceivable that the bankruptcy of ideas or of so-called serious-ness in the theatre has been, to a degree, a bankruptcy of method, which began when intellection became confused with the vending of specific solutions That the solutions have not worked out very well is no reason why the intellect must abdicate from the theatre. Nor is there any reason to seek the tether of uncritical traditionalism, by prescript from Eliot or anyone else. Because the freedom of modernism led the playwright, as well as his fellow-citizens, into error is no reason for replacing inquiry with dogma. It would be better to reflect that in so far as realism erred egregiously in opinion, it did so because it became dogmatic rather than critical, prescriptive rather than exploratory.

Finally, if the playwright is so inclined, he may endeavor to write poetic drama, whether formally in prose or verse. There may well be a future for poetic drama, if it serves to illuminate modern life rather than to obscure it with windy exclamations or obscurantist metaphysics. The poet, besides, needs a sterner discipline than he has generally had in view while working for the modern theatre. He should not rely on blank verse, for example, but on an idiom and meter attuned to contemporary speech. Nor should he mistake ornate rhetoric for dramatic poetry. The late critic Percy Hammond warned old-fashioned musical-comedy purveyors of high-kicking chorus girls that a knee was a joint and not an ornament. We may adapt this warning to poets who flourish and trumpet their poetry, although they need not go as far as does T. S. Eliot today in *concealing* it. For the contemporary theatre to be redeemed by poetry, dramatic conception must determine poetic expression. And there is little sense, of course, in inviting contemporary poets into the theatre unless they learn to communicate content without the help of exegesis, for which there is no time during a performance. The poet must become a dramatist if we are to have a sound alternative to dramatic realism. And in order to be meaningful to our stage, let him condescend to our common world a little. In aiming at universality, he should not rule out contemporary realities and become merely "historical." Lowes wisely declared that "there is nothing new that was not old." I believe it is necessary only to penetrate surfaces, even ordinary surfaces, in order to attain universality.

In conclusion, however, I realize that the future of both realism and poetry depends upon developments a critic can recommend but cannot ensure. Perhaps it would be best on this, as on other occasions, to let Bernard Shaw have the last word. "From time to time," Shaw wrote, "dramatic art gets a germinal impulse. There follows in the theatre a spring which flourishes into a glorious summer. This becomes stale almost before its arrival is generally recognized; and the sequel is not a new golden age, but a barren winter that may last any time from fifteen years to a hundred and fifty. Then comes a new impulse; and the cycle begins again." Let us hope that it will begin soon.

"WHY CAN'T THEY SAY
WHAT THEY MEAN?"

by Archibald MacLeish

They being, of course, the poets. Or rather, the contemporary poets—those who are now around. "Why can't they put it in so many words?" "Why can't they just come out with it?" There are various forms of the question and various tones of voice to ask it in—the indignant tone of the letter to the editor of the literary review, the contemptuous tone of the full-page institutional ad in the *New York Times* which bellows (lie quiet, ghosts of Avon and Weimar and Florence!) that the prime characteristic of a great work of art is to be easily understood, the earnest tone of the manifesto of the local poetry society, the outraged tone of the student who can't sit there silent any longer. But whatever the form and whatever the tone the intention is the same: "Why can't they say what they *mean*?" "Doesn't a poet need to be read?" demanded a student of mine in the blazing first paragraph of a paper on Pound's *Hugh Selwyn Mauberley*. "If not, what is the purpose of poetry? Art must be amazed at what some people do to attain her!"

No humane man can be indifferent to such a cry as that even when it leaves him with a lecture to write over. At least *I* cannot be indifferent, for its anguish takes me where I live. Not only am I a practitioner of the art of poetry and contemporary to the extent of being still alive: I am also, in a sense, a teacher of the art. That is to say that I spend a considerable part of my time attempting to teach young men and young women, not how to write poetry—no one, I think, would serious-

33

ly undertake to do that—but how to read it. The angrily held
conviction, therefore, that one of the most characterisic of
contemporary poems is not only unreadable but not seriously
to be read is, to me, a matter of concern. When I reflect, as I
must, that this conviction is not peculiar to one student in
one college but may be held by many students in many institutions, including, conceivably, the University of Michigan
itself, the concern becomes an active anxiety.

And an anxiety of a rather disturbing kind. I am not anxious
only for the intelligence of the rebellious student—he happened,
as a matter of fact, to be one of the most intelligent members
of his class. Neither am I fearful for the reputations of my
contemporaries among American and English poets. They have
done quite well in spite of the revolt and it is at least arguable
that some of them have flourished because of it. What disturbs
me is the relation of all this to what can only be called the
health of our civilization. A civilization without a poetry of its
own is a contradiction in terms, and a civilization which rejects
a poetry it has itself produced is sick: it is an Oedipus civilization stabbing at its own eyes. We may not like the kind of
poetry we have produced in the West in this century. We may
wish it were some other kind of poetry. But the fact is that
this poetry exists and that it is ours. And the further fact is
that if we lose contact with it we shall lose an essential contact
with ourselves. Only *this* poetry can give us to see that aspect
of our lives which poetry in any generation makes visible.
When the poetry produced by a particular kind of sensibility
is obscure to those to whom the sensibility belongs, the sensibility is obscure also—and the life out of which that sensibility
has developed.

If this seems to imply that obscurity in poetry is, at bottom,
a reader's problem rather than a writer's, I should have to
agree that it means just that. Where the obscurity complained
of is obscurity in an achieved work it is the reader, not the
writer, who must deal with it. Gide's observation that "obscurity
is something the true poet should neither seek nor fear" carries
the necessary corollary that obscurity is something the true

reader must neither evade nor avoid: he cannot reject the poem merely because he finds it obscure without failing in his reader's duty to the art.

This does not mean, of course, that there are not forms of obscurity which justify the rejection of a poem. Gide makes it plain that his remark applies to "true poets" only. The poet who is obscure because he is incapable of accomplishing understanding, or who is obscure because he is afraid of being understood, is not a true poet and should be judged accordingly. If a man *cannot* write clean English, or if he affects, by calculated dubieties, meanings of which his intelligence is incapable, he deserves no one's serious consideration. There is, however, all the difference in the world between the writer who deliberately contrives ambiguities in the hope of hoisting himself into significance, not by his own petard but by the chances of the dictionary, and the true poet who is obscure, or seems so, because of the controlled and achieved and intended implications of his work. With the true poet, obscurity, where it exists, is the condition of the poem and must be accepted by the reader in that sense. If the accomplished poem of the true poet is worth reading—we would agree, I suppose, that it must be— it is worth reading with its density upon it, for its density is part of what it is.

But to say so much is not, of course, to dispose of the problem. The obscurity, if there is obscurity, remains—and all the darker because the reader must stand before it alone. What is he to do about it? The answer depends, of course, on what his difficulty is and only he himself can tell us that. Let us therefore put the question to ourselves. What *is* this contemporary obscurity of which we so persistently complain when we speak of our own poets? Is it something more than mere difficulty of interpretation? If so, what? When the student rages or the respectable lady in the correspondence column spits, is it merely because the reading of this poetry is hard, or is it something else the protestants have in mind? Take Yeats for example. Is Yeats "obscure" within our contemporary usage of that word? Certainly "Byzantium" is as difficult as it is great, which means very difficult indeed. I have spent months over its reading in the past and I have no doubt I shall spend further months before I die. But is "Byzantium" *obscure*? Are any of Yeats's greatest poems *obscure*?

Not, I think, if one means by the word an obduracy which will not yield to ordinary intelligence and perceptiveness. One of Yeats's less important poems, a lyric from *Words For Music Perhaps* which has discouraged many readers, may serve us here:

HIS CONFIDENCE

Undying love to buy
I wrote upon
The corners of this eye
All wrongs done.
What payment were enough
For undying love?

I broke my heart in two
So hard I struck.
What matter? for I know
That out of rock,
Out of a desolate source
Love leaps upon its course.

There is not a single word here which is not readily readable nor is the syntax in any way complicated. What troubles those readers who experience trouble is apparently the images and the implications. Writing "all wrongs done" upon "the corners of this eye" strikes them as meaningless. But the meaning, however dark it may be to the intellect, is perfectly available to the image-reading imagination, is it not? The imagination knows that it is in the corner of the eye that the wrinkles of suffering are written. Once that is perceived the first stanza reads itself. I suffered wrongs willingly to buy what I hoped would be undying love for which no payment would be too great.

What then of the second stanza? Here again the only problem is that of the image and here again the image presents itself to the eye that can see. The heart is struck so hard that it breaks as one might strike and break a rock—as Moses struck the rock from which water gushed forth in that wilderness. Only here what gushes forth from the rock of the heart—from that desolate source—is love: love that leaps upon its course.

How then does the second stanza relate to the first? There is no syntactical connection, but the connection of emotional relationship is obvious enough. I had hoped to buy love *for* myself—undying love—by suffering: I did not succeed but by this suffering I broke my heart, and from my broken heart—that desolate source—poured forth *my* love. It is a small poem but a poem profoundly and unforgettably true, not only of Yeats and his unhappy love, out of which came so much else that leaped upon its course—poetry—insight, but of many, many others also: indeed, in some measure, of all of us.

The difficulty in reading "His Confidence," in other words, is in no way to be distinguished from the difficulty of reading a sonnet by Shakespeare or one of the odes of John Keats. And the same thing is true of Yeats's greatest poems also. Indeed Yeats differs from his comparable predecessors in two ways only: in his use of particular symbols and metaphors provided by his personal philosophic system, and in the special character of the critical apparatus which has grown up around his poems. The symbols and metaphors, however, create philosophical rather than poetic problems: they are *poetically* comprehensible in their own right and the philosophic significances can usually be ignored for reading purposes. As for the critical apparatus, it need not interfere unduly with the pleasure of reading Yeats. It is true of Yeats's work as of the work of many of his contemporaries that interpreters have sometimes increased the poetic difficulties in order to increase the academic triumphs, but the general reader is under no obligation to accept professional estimates of the hardships and adversities. Yeats's poems are poems, not puzzles, and the academic tendency to make riddles of them should not delude nor discourage the reader

who comes to them as works of art. He should remember that
"difficult" poets, or poets who can be made to seem so, are
godsends to the unpoetical instructor—which is why so many
courses, miscalled courses in modern poetry, are devoted to
their work: the instructor can teach the difficulties, not the
poems—a far easier task. With Yeats, as with all true artists,
it is the poems which matter.

And Yeats's poems are, to an unusual degree, whole and
complete within themselves, requiring nothing of their readers
—if we may call it nothing—but the power to see and hear and
feel and smell and taste and, above all, think. Misinterpreta-
tion comes when it does come, not from ignorance of the glosses
but from a failure to understand the syntax (which, in Yeats,
is as powerful as it is subtle), or from a failure to be *present*
sensuously and imaginatively at the scene, or from a failure to
exercise the full power of the intelligence in relating the experience of the poem to one's own experience of the world.
None of these things are easy to do in a poem like "Byzantium"
or "Vacillation" or "Among School Children" or "The Statues,"
but the difficulties in the way are not difficulties which anyone,
I think, could properly call obscurities. A work of art is not
obscure, as I understand the usage of the word, if it demands
of its readers or listeners or observers that they come to it fully
awake and in the possession of all their faculties. It is obscure
only if it demands of them what their faculties at their best
and liveliest cannot provide.

No, what the assailants of contemporary poetry have in mind is
not the difficulty of inward meaning one finds in Yeats. At
least it is not Yeats they mention. Their principal target is and
has been for many years Ezra Pound, and if there is one thing
more than another which is patently true of Ezra Pound it is
the fact that the meanings of *his* meanings are not in doubt.
His diagnosis of his time and of all previous times in his
Cantos comes down to the simplest of propositions—that usury
is the mother of all ill. His ideas about literature—and they are
numerous—are as definite and precise, and as fruitful, as ideas

could well be. And his emotions, at least the emotions his
poetry expresses, are as plain as they are few:

> Tard, trés tard, je t'ai connue, la Tristesse,
> I have been hard as youth sixty years.

> J'ai eu pitié des autres
> probablement pas assez, and at moments that
> suited my convenience.

It is accurately said. Love of dead men and women you will
find in Pound, but for the living—including, at the last, himself
—little but exasperation or contempt or rage. It is not, therefore, because his intentions are dark that Pound can be charged
with obscurity. It is for another and a wholly different reason—
a reason which may go some way to elucidate the nature of
the whole complaint about contemporary poetry.

What brings the charge of obscurity down upon Ezra
Pound is the *character of the references* to persons and to
events out of which he constructs the fabric of his more
important work. The beginning of the Sixth Canto will serve
as an example:

> What you have done, Odysseus,
>   We know what you have done. . .
> And that Guillaume sold out his ground rents
> (Seventh of Poitiers, Ninth of Aquitain).
> 'Tant las fotei com auzirets
>   'Cen e quatre vingt et veit vetz . . .'
> The stone is alive in my hand, the crops
>   will be thick in my death-year . . .

Who, says the indignant reader, is this William? And what was
seventh of Poitiers and ninth of Aquitaine? And why ground
rents? And what is this Provençal couplet about making love
to somebody a hundred and eighty-four times? And in whose
hand is the stone alive? And what stone? And what is the

relation between the live stone and the thick crops and the death year? And who am "I" who suddenly appears at the end? And why—a thousand times why—go at it in this way anyhow?

Well, the answers to the first seven questions can be quite accurately supplied if anyone is willing to take the trouble. A Mr. Carne-Ross was, with the following results: William is William IX of Aquitaine (d. 1127), crusader and troubadour, who sold his lands to tenants instead of hiring them out and thus living by "usury," and the couplet is from one of William's poems in which he boasts of having spent eight days incognito with two noble ladies who believed he was dumb and wouldn't be able to tell anybody (with the frequent consequences aforesaid), and the thick crops refer to the fruitful results throughout the kingdom of so much royal potency, and the stone alive in the hand, orchidaceous pun aside, refers to the fact that the arts of the stonecutter and the builder, like all the rest of the arts, flourish under a potent father-king as distinguished from an impotent usurer-king. All of which, of course, makes complete sense as well as establishing the fundamental truth in view: that everything does well, including, presumably, the two noble ladies, where wealth isn't hired. The last question however still remains. Why go at it this way? Why not say it in so many words? Why, in any event, not put it all down so that it can be understood without the assistance of such scholars and interpreters as the ingenious Mr. Carne-Ross?

But here again our guide has gone before us. The fault, says Mr. Carne-Ross, is in ourselves, not in Mr. Pound. Mr. Pound should not be denounced because we can't take his broad hints and reconstruct an entire corner of history out of a man's name and a tag of Provençal verse. The trouble is that we have lost the common heritage of myth and legend to which earlier and more fortunate writers could appeal and have become incompetent readers. No one is to blame but the generations which broke the tradition and the only remedy, if we wish to read again, is to shore up the shattered columns and rebuild the city.

It is not, I think you will agree, a very comforting or a very persuasive answer. It is quite true that Milton made copious use of curious names and events which his readers were able to identify only because they and he had read the same books and studied the same languages. It is true also that all those elder poets who constructed their poetic world out of classic mythology or ancient history or the tales of Boccaccio found ready readers only because their generation knew Boccaccio and the myths as well as they. But are Guillaume and his couplet really of that order? Was there ever a time when an English poet could expect to be generally understood in such terms? And Pound—let there be no mistake about that—does wish to be understood: ". . . in discourse," he says in his Seventy-ninth Canto, "what matters is/to get it across e poi basta." Indeed the aim of writing, as his Eightieth Canto sees it, is "to bring your g.r. to the nutriment/gentle reader to the gist of the discourse."

No, the problem is considerably more complicated and more interesting than Mr. Carne-Ross makes it seem. Pound's references in his *Cantos* are drawn from the poetry and art and politics of a dozen languages and countries and there has never been a "common heritage of myth and legend" in English, or, I think, in any other tongue, which contained anythink like thàt body of public knowledge. Nor has any "common heritage of myth and legend" in any country ever contained the *kind* of recondite or purely personal or purely scholarly allusion to which Pound is prone. Take, for example, the First Canto with its magnificently cadenced account of the voyage of Odysseus from Circe's island to that beach in Hell: the strong pull of the rhythm when the wind takes hold of the ship and the levelling off after, like the levelling off of the vibrations of a climbing plane, when the sail truly fills and the ship runs in the open sea. Towards the end of this Canto, after an extended passage which would be wholly intelligible to anyone who knew Homer, and readable enough whether one knew Homer or not, there suddenly appears a character named Divus (patently no Greek) who is commanded to lie quiet, and, beside him, a "Cretan" of whom nothing is said but that an unspecified "phrase" is his. Their position in the Canto indicates that they are persons of importance but nothing in the Canto itself identifies them, nor is there anything in the common heritage of the English-speaking peoples either now or at any previous time which would enable a reader to discover who they are or why they are there. As a matter of fact, only Pound himself, or a sedulous student who had read Pound's other writings, or, conceivably, a specialist in late Latin texts, should such a man take to reading contemporary poetry, could very well know the necessary answer. For Andreas Divus was a scholar who lived early in the sixteenth century and wrote a Latin translation of the Odyssey, "little more than a trot or a pony," which Pound, as he tells us in an essay of 1918, had picked up in a Paris bookstall about 1908 or 1910 in an edition of the early 1800's which contained also the *Hymni Deorum* of a certain Cretan named Georgius Dartona, the second of which (to Aphrodite) contained, in turn, the phrase here suggested. And why is Divus to lie quiet? Because the preceding matter is largely a translation, or rather a magnificent transubstantiation, of his text.

Now this, you may very well think, is a special and understandable case: an ingenious method of at once confessing and concealing plagiarism. It is, I assure you, no such thing. To begin with, Divus, not Pound, is the beneficiary of this traffic as the great translator—for Pound is surely one of the greatest in the history of our tongue—very well knew. Again, and more important, Divus and the Cretan are not isolated instances. They are two among multitudes in the *Cantos* and elsewhere. The Second Canto, the most lyrical of the lot, contains, for example, in the midst of such a Mediterranean scene as no other modern poet has accomplished, "the voice of Schoeney's daughters." You find there Sordello, whom even an age which has forgotten Browning remembers; you find Eleanor of Aquitaine—no problem surely; you find Homer—"Ear, ear for the sea-surge, murmur of old men's voices"; you find Helen; you find Tyro whom any classical dictionary will identify as the beautiful daughter of the King of Elis who was seduced by Neptune as she walked by the river bank

> And the blue-grey glass of the wave tents them,
> Glare azure of water, cold-welter, close cover . . .;

you have the Mediterranean full of light and dazzle with [Pound's phrases] the quiet sun-tawny sand-stretch and the gulls broading out their wings in the sun and the snipe coming for their bath, spreading wet wings to the sun film; you have evening and that tower like a one-eyed great goose craning up out of the olives "And the frogs singing against the fauns/in the half light";—you have all this, and in the middle of it you have the voice of Schoeney's daughters. And who are Schoeney's daughters? How can a man discover them? Only by reading Golding's translation of Ovid, which few have read and none can now buy, where it is written:

> Atlant, a goodlie lady, one
> of Schoeney's daughters.

Atlanta and her sisters stand alone in their private darkness amidst all that light, but not so the rest of the masked figures of Pound's poems. As you read on into the later *Cantos* the masks crowd around you until, in the Pisan group, the naked face is the exception. Only a reader who was himself present in the Disciplinary Barracks of the American Army at Pisa during the months of Pound's incarceration there could possibly identify the greater part of the shadowy figures of that Inferno: could possibly know, for example, that the roster of Presidents of the United States refers to a list of Negro prisoners, or that the Steele of "Steele that is one awful name" identifies the officer in command of the stockade. The references here are not only outside any common cultural heritage: they are outside the possibilities of common knowledge of any kind. Only with the aid of commentators and interpreters—very spe-

cial commentators and interpreters—can they be read at all and
some references have thus far mystified even the most devoted
of the glossarists. The world still waits, I believe, for the identification of a certain nobleman with dirty lace cuffs who pops
up out of nowhere in the Café Dante in Verona.

Now, the cumulative effect of all this is, without doubt,
infuriating. Even so wise and gentle a man as that fine Greek
poet, George Seferis, betrays irritation when he thinks back over
his experience of the *Cantos:* "The reader turning the pages becomes dizzy noting the successive insertions of foreign texts;
of incidents or of conversations, very often in a foreign language; of persons known from history or entirely unknown,
whose unexpected presence he cannot explain . . ." The irritation is understandable. But is irritation or even rage an adequate answer to the puzzle? Is it really enough to say, as a
very considerable number of our contemporaries do say, that
you "can't read" Pound—or "can't read" contemporary poetry
in general because of Pound; that its obscurities are unnecessary; that they could easily be dispensed with; that the whole
thing is a fraud? Here is a man whose position as "true poet"
is not open to question: Eliot gave it as his opinion some years
ago that Pound was then the most important poet writing in
English. Here, furthermore, is a man whose declared purpose
as a poet is to communicate: a man to whom the first law of
discourse is to communicate *e poi basta.* Is it possible to dismiss the work of such a man as deliberately dark or intentional-
ly obscure or merely incompetent? Is it conceivable that a
writer of this stature and these beliefs would devote his life
and his art to frustration or could, without adequate reason,
construct so curious a monument to himself?

And yet what reason can there be for the use by any writer,
no matter what his position or his convictions, of a vocabulary
of reference which no one but himself or his coterie or some
desperate candidate for the Ph.D. can ever be expected to
unravel? How can Pound feel obliged to represent essential
parts of what he has to say not by common but by proper
nouns, unknown as well as known; by fragments of quotations

in numerous tongues, including tongues neither the writer
nor his readers speak; by fragments of history as it was or as
it might have been, either in his own country or in some
other; by bits of conversation between unrecognized conver-
sationalists; by the dry feathers and old tags of the gossip of the
art studios? Why doesn't he come straight out with it in com-
prehensive and comprehensible words? Why, in brief, doesn't
he say what he means?

The question with which we started has, you see, somewhat
altered its character. What began as an irritable complaint about
the habits and practices of contemporary poets as a group has
become a disturbed and rather disturbing inquiry into the
reasons for the behavior of one of them. Unless we are prepared to assert, as no intelligent man could, that Pound's
principal poems are a vast and foolish hoax, we must consider
that their method has a purpose. But what purpose?

A specific example, taken from Pound's finest poem, *Hugh
Selwyn Mauberley,* may perhaps make the question more
precise. In the first section of *Mauberley,* the Ode, which sums
up the dilemma of the literary young man whose literary fate is
to be the subject of the sequence, there occurs the line

His true Penelope was Flaubert.

Here, of five words, two are proper nouns, but proper nouns in
this case with which any intelligent reader will be familiar.
Penelope is of course the beloved to whom through thick or
thin a wanderer returns. Flaubert is a novelist whose theories of
style and whose handling of experience altered the course not
only of the novel but of the art of letters generally. What is
being said, then, to the reader who understands these references,
is that a certain literary style and attitude were the end and
object of someone's searchings—in this case Hugh Selwyn
Mauberley's. But this is being said not in several dozen
words but in five, and with a gain, not a loss, of allusiveness
and precision. Pound's line is far more meaningful than my

paraphrase, as well as being briefer, handsomer, and more memorable. And the same thing is true, it will be found, throughout this remarkable poem. Very little of *Mauberley* is *about* its subject: the greater part of it *is* its subject. The poem is less a poem, in the ordinary sense, than a detailed tapestry made up of proper names and the figures they evoke; made up of moments of past time, of gods, of mottoes, of landscapes. Where a literary generalization would have been possible, there is Flaubert *tout court*. Where Mauberley's frenzied pride is in issue there, instead of the appropriate epithet, is Capaneus on the walls of Thebes. Where it is Mauberley's gullibility which is to be exposed there is no adjective, there is only the image of the trout and its factitious bait. The figure takes the place of the abstraction.

But what then is this figured writing? How, except in its own terms, is it to be described? In an age in which every other book is a book about symbolism, are we to call these figures symbols? Not certainly in any sense but Suzanne Langer's, to whom everything that means is so defined. These are rather *signs* than symbols. They stand, not, as Yeats's symbols do, for the invisible essence which only this particular visible form can express, but for general ideas or conceptions which general terms could also have communicated. The particular is chosen *instead* of the general: the figure *in place* of the abstraction.

What we have, in other words, as a number of recent writers on Pound have helpfully pointed out, is a kind of picture writing. The common coinage of familiar discursive writing in which the same word may serve a multitude of different uses, designating now one particular event and now another, is rejected wherever possible in favor of a series of unique and specific words designating unique and specific situations. As in the case of picture writing, the number of signs is limitlessly increased, but each sign belongs much more nearly to its thing than in the case of signs made out of the interchangeable terms of the generalizing dictionary. One critic of Pound's work has referred to his figures as pictograms or ideograms, but they are much more specific than that. Ideograms have also, in their way and within their limits, exchangeable meanings: Pound's figures have not. The figure of the line "His true Penelope was Flaubert" is not pictogram Flaubert set down beside pictogram Penelope in associated conjunction. The figure is Flaubert *and* Penelope; Flaubert *in the context of* Penelope; Flaubert, if you will, in Penelope's dress.

We could multiply instances throughout *Mauberley* and the *Cantos,* but the situation is, I think, clear. *The obscurity of which complaint is made in Pound is an obscurity of the specific.* His meanings are dark because he composes in pictures and because his pictures are sometimes, like private photographs, too peculiarly unique; because the particular figure does not signify to all, or, in extreme cases, to any, of Pound's readers. Here is somebody in *Mauberley* whom an expert on the generals of the Franco-German War might recognize as one of them—though even he might well be wrong. Here in the *Cantos* is what may be a Chinese god or a Chinese girl or even a Chinese philosopher: only a Taoist would know, and not many Taoists read Pound. Here is "Poor Jenny" whom no one but the Pre-Raphaelites would recall—and the Pre-Raphaelites are dead. The figures are meaningful enough—specifically and wonderfully meaningful—when they are identified, but until we can place these ambiguous figures they are so many faces in a heap of faces signifying nothing, and our question repeats itself with point and passion: Why not *say* it in general and generally comprehensible terms? Why hand us the private photographs to figure out if we can?

Pound, if we asked him—if we looked back through his theories and his theorizing—would tell us something by way of answer but not enough. For years in his younger days he went about London attacking English poets of renown as fabricators of a mere "vehicle for transmitting thoughts" and demanding the substitution of what he called "specific rendering." Now "rendering" is a Symbolist word of the nineties and we may look to Symbolist doctrine to define its meaning. To the Symbolists the poet's business was with his experience, and particularly with the experience of his consciousness, and every moment of that experience was unique. It was therefore the poet's task to invent a particular language appropriate to his particular life. What was basic to Symbolist doctrine, in other words, was the diversity of experience, and what Pound was doing in his early days in London was to carry Symbolist doctrine to its logical conclusion: the conclusion that diversity of experience must be expressed in diversity of terms. If you can't generalize experience neither can you generalize *about* experience. All you can do is "render" it "explicitly" in its inherent explicitness, placing your reader where you yourself have been—naked among the minute particulars. Literature to Pound, as every fortunate school boy has now been taught, is language "charged with meaning" to the greatest possible extent, and the greatest possible extent is the extent made possible by "explicit rendering."

That is the theory. But face to face with a poem we cannot read because the explicitness of the rendering is explicit in terms of someone or something we can't identify, the theory does not help us very much. It does not resolve the obscurity. If anything the obscurity resolves *it*. The poem stands there meaningless for all the talk, and we are suddenly given to see that the theory is merely what literary theories so often are— an excuse and a self-justification. Pound has made a virtue, as the Symbolists before him made a virtue, of rejecting the generalization, the least common denominator, and presenting the unique and diverse and fragmented experience in equivalents of itself. But in so doing he has quite obviously been driven, as the virtue-makers commonly are, by something other than literary choice—by an unnamed literary necessity. "Explicit rendering" is not inevitably and always a good thing in itself. It may produce marvellously precise and moving effects when its explicit equivalents are legible, but when they are not legible it may produce no effects at all. And it is quite obvious that they must often be illegible. There are simply not enough publicly recognizable photographs in any man's bureau drawer to enable him to present an extensive or complicated experience by this means.

The theory therefore fails to justify the obscurity of which we complain: we must go beyond the choice to the necessity. We must go to the reasons which produced the theory. We must ask why, granted that "explicit rendering" is not always and under all circumstances a better way of writing poetry, Pound was obliged to persuade himself and others that it was? Why was it impossible for him to employ those readier means of communication which had been open to poets, including the greatest poets, in the past? When anything happened to Goethe, as Gide once remarked, he turned it into a generality. Why could not Pound?

The answer—and it is an answer which has much to say about the whole question of obscurity of reference in contemporary poetry—is, I think, this: *Neither Pound nor his contemporaries have been able to turn the particular into the general as Goethe did because the general is not available to them as it was a hundred years before.* Goethe's was a time in which the particular found its place in the general naturally and easily and was best observed in that context. Ours is a time of a very different character. The "general order," if there is one, is no longer open to serious writers in prose or verse, and the particular is so overwhelming in its particularity that it can only be understood, when it can be understood at all, in its character as itself. The consequence is that our literature has of necessity become a literature of particularity. In prose we have been forced toward that particularity of the external world which we call "realism," or toward that other inward particularity which attempts to present the moments of the individual consciousness in their ungeneralized and ungeneralizable diversities. Poetry, moved by the same influences, has been driven in the same direction. But because the end and purpose of poetry is not merely to represent or to comprehend experience but to *possess* it, "realism" of whichever kind has not served as the poetic means. Poetry has been driven not merely to *designate* the particulars but, in some way, to *contain* them. The labor is not new in kind. Thousands of years before our epoch it was practiced by Chinese poets in their

attempts to possess isolated moments of experience. What is
new with us is the application of the method. Ours are the
first poets in the history of the art to attempt to use the poetry
of specific equivalents for such extended renderings of public
experience as Eliot's vision of the modern world in *The Waste
Land* or Pound's view of universal history in *The Cantos.*

The essential point, however, so far as their obscurity goes,
is not that our poets have made the attempt. The essential
point is that the attempt has been forced upon them. Lacking
a "general order" to contain the great sequences of time and
space and to provide metaphors for their expression, our contemporaries have had no alternative, if they wished to handle
those sequences, but to represent them in their specific equivalents. The obscurity of reference in contemporary poetry, in
other words, is truly an obscurity of necessity rather than of
choice. If it is not, for that reason, less obscure, it is, or should
be, less offensive. A reader who feels that difficulties have
been deliberately thrown in his way in accordance with some
aesthetic doctrine or other, has occasion to feel indignant: a
reader who understands that the difficulties he faces are difficulties inherent in the approach to the experience he is attempting to possess, has none. If labor is demanded of him it
is labor imposed not by the whim of the poet but by the
necessities of the poet's task.

This is not to argue that all the difficulties of reference in
modern poetry are inescapable. The greatest of modern poets,
Yeats, succeeded in forcing the most characteristic of all contemporary experiences to express itself in terms and images
which any reader with the least awareness of himslf and of
his world can comprehend. There can hardly be a student in
any American college worthy of the name to whom *The
Second Coming* is not a meaningful statement. But the fact
that other contemporary poets have not achieved Yeats's mastery of the experience of the age does not mean that their
work is not essential to an understanding of the sensibility of
our time, or, what is perhaps more important, to its expression.
Those readers who have come to see that poetry is an instru-

ment of knowledge, and that the knowledge it can convey is a knowledge of their own lives, and that their own lives must be lived in the age into which they have been born, will not willingly be excluded from the poetry of their own time by those difficulties of communication which are a characteristic of the time and a condition of its experience.

CRITICISM AND THE IMAGINATION
OF ALTERNATIVES

by Philip Rahv

It has been repeatedly observed of late that the period we are living in is far better endowed critically than creatively, and it is certainly true that in recent years we have witnessed an unprecedented rise in critical activity. Moreover, critics have become so self-conscious of what they are about as to engage in intensive examinations of their discipline, its uses and abuses, methods, assumptions, and purposes. This is all to the good, no doubt, in so far as it may bring forth a wider and keener appreciation of the true nature and proper employment of the critical medium.

Yet, for all its busyness, contemporary criticism exhibits certain features, among which is a peculiar and increasing self-sufficiency setting it apart somewhat from the literary process as a whole, that cannot but arouse misgivings. The truth is that this busyness of criticism has fallen short of bracing us intellectually or of producing those tonic qualities the want of which is so acutely felt in our literary situation. For one thing, though criticism is apparently thriving, new imaginative writing is for the most part stricken with a sluggishness of spirit quite untypical of the modern enterprise in letters; and this condition may well indicate a growing derangement of the normal relation between the critical and creative faculties in our literary economy. For another, criticism in this period impresses one as being controlled by rather narrow assumptions. The incentive is mainly pedagogic, with far too much concern with the quasi mysteries of "methodology" and not nearly enough release of the energy of discovery—the kind of energy which William James once identified as "the imagination of alternatives." My object in this paper is, first, to explore some of the ways in which that type of imagination might affect our ideas of criticism and, second, to inquire into some of the causes operative in our time that have exalted criticism to its present position.

Two such causal factors suggest themselves to me. One is local and the other more general in character. The local factor, which surely accounts in part at least for the present display of critical energy, arises, I think, from the migration of writers into the academy that has occurred in the past few decades. This migration is quite as much a socio-esthetic as it is a socio-economic phenomenon. It is changing some of the essentials of American literary life, and among the changes it has already enforced is a rise in the prestige of criticism. For the writer-teacher is likely to be concerned less with the social and historical background of literary creation than with its intrinsic qualities and effects; he is therefore inclined to insist on the distinction between the actual merit of a work of literature and its historical importance. But this amalgamation of criticism with teaching is by no means a one-sided process. If criticism changes teaching so does teaching change criticism by providing it with a more solid institutional basis than it disposed of in the past.

Certainly the emergence of the movement known as the "new criticism" is scarcely to be understood apart from this migration of writers into the universities and the consequent clash that has ensued between old and new methods of imparting literary knowledge. Thus on one side at least the "new criticism" essentially represents an effort to redefine the relationship between literature and the academy, or, more specifically, to meet the need that has arisen to replace past methods of teaching literary texts with a more adequate method, taking full account of the critical function. Inevitably this has exposed the "new criticism" to a double attack, coming on the one hand from old-time professors of English, prone to dismiss it as mere literature, and on the other from old-time literary men who make out that it amounts to no more than "the simple annotation of classroom texts." Exaggerated as this latter charge may be, it is certainly true that the typical tone and style of the younger generation of "new critics"—the generation, that is, whose career does not go so far back as the 1920's and whose experience of literary life is almost entirely restricted to the academy—are unmistakably those of an address to students rather than to the general reader. The devices most favored by the younger critics in organizing material, such as the deliberately slow pace, the patient concentration on textual minutiae, the cautious progression from item to item, and, above all, the avoidance of general ideas and of the larger and more controversial issues, immediately suggest the classroom approach rather than the synoptic mode that forms the traditional resource of critical expression in its greater moments.

We would do well to distinguish between the literary character of such older writers as Eliot, Pound, Richards, Empson, Tate, Ransom, Blackmur, Winters, Austin Warren, and Robert Penn Warren (the founding fathers, so to speak, of the "new criticism") and that of their younger disciples. The former, coming out of a different and more seminal cultural period, are all intractably their own men and possessed of richly diversified interests. It is the younger generation really who at present compose a school of "new critics" *tout court*. This school has now settled down to its tasks, and what it appears to stand for mainly is the academic consolidation of the "revolution in poetry" which took place in the English-speaking world between 1910 and 1930 approximately and which is principally linked in our minds with the names of Eliot and Pound. The "new criticism" is thus a meaningful term historically in so far as it refers to a grouping of critics formed some decades ago, most of them also practicing poets, who were predominantly concerned with demonstrating the significance of modern poetry by revaluating the order of English poetry as a whole. That mission has been triumphantly accomplished. But in the "new criticism" as currently expounded there is another element, and that is the traditionalist ideology taken over almost exclusively from Eliot. This element strikes one as problematical, to say the least, and for my part I cannot see that its connection with the central poetic doctrine with which it is usually combined is more than fortuitous. Traditionalism is after all but one ideology among many, and as such its degree of truth or falsity is not to be determined on literary grounds alone.

Clearly, the partnership that criticism has newly effected with teaching has influenced it in ways both positive and negative. The positive aspect is to be noted in the distinct gains that criticism has made in prestige, morale, and productivity. The negative aspect is that, in becoming overtly pedagogic, criticism runs the risk of cutting itself off from the creative writer as well as from the general reader, who not unexpectedly is seldom in a mood to go back to school. "Criticism is the very education of our imaginative life," as Henry James so handsomely defined it; in the Jamesian context, however, the word "education" must be taken in a sense more honorific than literal. Education is primarily a matter of institutional practice, while criticism has by and large functioned as a free medium of literary expression and judgment.

In a notable essay in *The Sacred Wood* T. S. Eliot once defined what he named as "the essentially uncritical state"; and among the ways of reaching that state he singled out that of regarding literature as an institution—"accepted, that is to say, with the same gravity as the establishments of Church and State." Now this is an unfortunate state of mind which criticism in its present mood can scarcely be said to resist with sufficient force. Indeed, not a few of our critic-teachers have lately taken to celebrating the institutional aspects of literature. But the sense in which literary art can be described as an institution is at bottom no more than a paltry truism. Institutions are not only inevitable but necessary. Art too cannot escape the bonds they impose; nor would we want it to escape such bonds and attain a condition of unqualified liberty. Yet to join in solemnizing the institutional aspects of art is gratuitous at best. It is far more refreshing to attest to the fact that art has nearly always been much too restive to have acquired very reliable institutional manners and uses; that in a certain sense art is actually the great counterforce to institutions, in that it cannot without self-betrayal be ultimately reconciled to their rigidity and impersonality.

So far I have touched only upon the local or national circumstances affecting the status of criticism. The other factor involved is far more general in character. I have in mind the enormous growth in self-consciousness that we have been witnessing for many years now in the practice of all artistic media, and our increasing and well-nigh irresistible inclination to achieve a rational, that is, a critical understanding of all artistic means, conventions, rules, and traditions. What this comes to, of course, is a kind of historical loss of innocence, making for an incursion of critique into the creative act itself. In an essay written soon after the last war, Ernst Robert Curtius, the outstanding German critic and scholar, spoke in glowing terms of this growing self-consciousness and expansion of the critical faculty, for in his opinion this expansion was bringing about a union of creative intuition and analytical intelligence.

> We must throw off [he wrote] the superstition that poets must be simple-minded, that literary men are necessarily uneducated. . . . T. S. Eliot interests me all the more for combining critique and poetry in his own person. He reinforces my conviction . . . that in the twentieth century criticism has become a leading component of all higher spiritual and intellectual production. You ask for examples? Here they are: Gide, Proust, Valery, Joyce, Larbaud, Ayala, Ortega. . . . All are artists of intellectualism, all makers of consciousness. The capacity to shape material into artistic form . . . has ceased to be enough.

As an account of what has actually been happening in modern literature this is accurate enough. Still, I must confess that for me that last remark of Herr Curtius', namely that the capacity to shape material into artistic form has ceased to be enough, strikes a rather portentous note. To consider intellectualism as a positive good and nothing else is manifestly one-sided. There is another side to the equation, and that is the loss of spontaneity and consequent danger of sterility which is so often the unlooked-for outcome of the victorious investment of the creative act by the spirit of critique with its painful deliberateness and rationalizing of the imaginative grasp of experience. From another point of view, that of Thomas Mann, for instance, in his novel *Doctor Faustus,* this very growth of self-consciousness and proficiency in analysis is regarded as a symptom of decadence, imperiling the artist's chances of bringing his creative powers to full realization. The protagonist of Mann's novel, the composer Adrian Leverkuehn, sells his soul to the devil precisely because he stands in need of demonic assistance if he is to break through the control of his art by reason and thus find his way back to what he calls "the old primeval enthusiasm, the divine raptus, genuine inspiration, immediate, absolute, unquestioned, ravishing." Knowingly or not, Leverkuehn is here invoking the ancient theory of artistic creation as an act of inspiration to which consciousness has no access, the very theory which Socrates invoked when he contended that poets write poetry not by wisdom but by "a sort of genius and inspiration" that reminded him of diviners and soothsayers, who also say many fine things without understanding their meaning. It is curious to find Thomas Mann making the most of this ancient idea of art in depicting a modern predicament; and even if he may be said to have overdramatized it in his novel, his version of it will nevertheless do very well as a foil to Herr Curtius' contrary notion.

I have wanted to place the present-day workings of the critical faculty in a broad enough perspective to allow us to perceive what is at stake in its bid for influence and authority. For the more we become aware of the importance of criticism in our age, the more urgent the necessity of discriminating between the true and false alternatives open to it.

2

One of the major alternatives proposed to criticism is that it convert itself into a science of literature or at any rate into a discipline rigorous enough to justify its advancement to near-scientific status. Is this a meaningful ambition presenting criticism with a viable alternative? I think not. To be sure, there is a whole array of facts about literature that can be studied in a scientific manner more or less. But such studies belong chiefly to scholarship rather than to literary criticism properly speaking. Since criticism deals more with questions of value than with questions of fact, it is unlikely that it will ever be able so to transform itself in essence as to acquire even so much of objectivity as the social sciences lay claim to. Criticism seems inextricably bound up with issues of value, of belief and ideological conflict; and if we are not deluded by purely theoretical models of criticism but look to its actual practice in the past as in the present, we realize soon enough that the greater part of the criticism of consequence that we know is shot through and through with ideological motives and postulations that remain for the most part unanalyzed and unacknowledged.

Of course, once a given criticism has been completed in the sense of having been brought to its historical consummation, the student of it may well undertake to sort out the ideology it contains from other components that appear to him to have permanent validity. In fact, this sorting out is an activity that we pursue continually in our inspection of past criticism, and we may also attempt to cope in the same way with our contemporaries. However, this sorting out is essentially an *ex post facto* operation, performed not by the critic himself but by those coming after him; nor is there any certain method available to us insuring that such latecomers go about their task free of ideological presuppositions of their own. We may think that, for example, we have by now sorted out to our complete satisfaction Dr. Johnson's ideas concerning metaphysical poetry; yet in the future critics may conclude that our altered estimate of this poetry was not quite the act of superior critical discernment that we take it to be, but was fully as subject as Dr. Johnson's estimate was to the varying ideological pressures and provocations of the historical process. This does not necessarily mean that our judgment of metaphysical poetry will not be vindicated in the future. All it means, rather, is that the historical process may either weaken or strengthen our critical judgment, that it may work in our favor or against us; in other words, that as critics we never exercise our judgment in the perfection of self-determination but within an historically conditioned framework of cultural need and response.

The demand that is being made nowadays for a radical purification of criticism implies something quite unreal, namely that the literary interest can be advantageously divorced from other interests. Mr. F. R. Leavis has very effectively hit at this notion in remarking that "one cannot seriously be interested in literature and remain purely literary in interests." This he said in the course of questioning Ezra Pound's proposal that poetic technique be studied by itself, impersonally and in splendid isolation as it were, apart, that is, from the sensibility, with its varied and manifold content, engaged in applying that technique. Pound had proposed studying "how the pouring is done," and Leavis' retort was that "how the pouring is done cannot be studied apart from the thing poured. . . . We have to speak of technique as something distinct from sensibility, but technique can be studied and judged only in terms of the sensibility it expresses. The technique not studied as the expression of a particular sensibility is an unprofitable abstraction." Surely Leavis is entirely in the right in this matter. And, indeed, if we accept the premise that criticism is ever closely attendant upon sensibility, then we must give due weight to the fact that it invariably resists the effort to systematize it and to predict its development; and there is no science without system and prediction. For that matter, sensibility also resists the effort to institutionalize it. In this respect it has an affinity with love, of which Nietzsche once said that it is the one thing in the world which cannot be institutionalized.

Criticism, I take it, is a reflexive discourse of the literary mind, and it is very much a mixed discourse besides. And though the good critic knows that the mixing is inevitable, he is also possessed of sufficient intellectual tact and sense of relevance to know just how to mix and what to mix. Yet at the same time he is under no illusions that criticism can be subjected with any real hope of success to a strict delimitation of function and to a purge of its allegedly "extraliterary" interests. He cannot but regard any such notion as a Utopia of rationalism, growing out of the division of labor and the mania for specialization which are among the least attractive features of modern culture.

But if criticism is not a science, is it proper, then, to speak of it as a literary medium? I would say that it is exactly that in the strict sense of being a department of letters. It is not an artistic medium, however, and for my purpose the distinction between a literary and an artistic medium is worth stressing. A critical essay is not a work of art but neither is it a piece of purely objective writing, entirely informative or utilitarian in character. Being involved with the objects of sensibility, criticism necessarily adopts some of its means of expression, such as style and symbolic reference.

Having brought criticism so close to some of the primary processes of literature, I am tempted to proceed even further along the same lines. Is it not possible to maintain that the function of criticism is best understood in conceiving of it as a superstructural form of literature, its generalization into consciousness, or, to put it more directly, as a form of literature about literature? It depends on literature not only for its subject matter but also for its fundamental experience, and if it deals with life, as it is often brought to do, it does so at the remove of its esthetic incarnation in the basic literary genres. I am offering this idea of criticism not as a rigorous definition or conclusive theory of it but simply as a provisional approach and as a corrective to the fetishism of method to which the critical intelligence has lately been yielding.

The principal objection that presents itself is that in conceiving of criticism as a form of literature, even if only as a form of literature *about* literature, we are in effect abolishing its cognitive function. The critic is, after all, concerned for the most part with discovering and verifying truths about the literary process, while the creative writer is concerned with the invention and formal elaboration of fictions. To this objection the rejoinder would be that it is chiefly in the popular view that the fiction embodied in the poem, novel, or play is something wholly feigned or imagined which offers us the possibility of pleasurable identification at the price of untruth. If we reject, however, this vulgar view of the nature of the imaginative fiction, recognizing that it has a measure of cognitive value peculiar to itself and gained through its own proper means, then we can see our way clear to retaining the truths of criticism. For we can then put it that criticism has cognitive value in relation to literature to the degree, no more and no less, that literature can be said to have cognitive value in relation to life.

This conception of criticism has, to be sure, little to do with formal esthetic theorizing. It derives rather from the empirical observation of the behavior of criticism, its actual performance in the sphere of letters, and of the demeanor of the critic as a man of letters. Moreover this conception has in its favor the appeal of economy in that it reforges the unity of the literary mind, bringing its creative and critical faculties into close accord instead of disconnecting and driving them apart, as is being done nowadays by most theorists of the critical task.

To see criticism in its literary character is to realize that an exclusively valid method of work can no more be prescribed in its field than in poetry or the drama. Not that all methods are equally good. Some are obviously more rewarding than others, but this truism hardly comes to the same thing as the idea of salvation through method—a method single, strict, all-pertinent, and alone legitimate. Though this idea may appear to resolve some of the quandaries of criticism by normalizing it, in the long run it leaves it in a worse quandary than ever. In its way this idea is in itself an admission that the imagination of alternatives has failed us, that we are prepared to embrace a narrow specialization that may perhaps satisfy our sense of professional status and enhance our pride in it but only at the expense of the living man in us. In the present literary situation what the critic needs above all is to recover the role of participant in the literary event—a role that can again belong to him if he seizes it; and if nowadays he more often than not prefers to play the part of a disengaged spectator and analyst of the literary event, the reasons for such unheroic renunciation are not to be sought in the nature of criticism per se but in other spheres altogether.

The conception of criticism as a literary medium is a difficult one to sustain. I have discussed one major objection to it. Another one, not quite so telling, is that it makes criticism into a medium that has its end within itself. Now the dominant view has been that criticism, unlike the basic literary media, has no such autonomy; only a small minority of critics have maintained that in this respect too it differs hardly at all from literature in general. Thus John Middleton Murry contends that criticism performs the same function as literature itself, that of providing the critic with a means of expression; and Remy de Gourmont speaks of criticism as a subjective literary form, a perpetual confession on the critic's part. "The critic may think," he writes, "that he is judging the work of other people, but it is himself that he is revealing and exposing to the public." Needless to say, this is a notion I do not subscribe to. In my understanding of criticism, it is a medium first and foremost of the critic's response to literature and only indirectly, by refraction as it were, of his response to life.

It seems possible to transcend these contrary views of criticism by going beyond the particular formulations given them. May we not say that subjectively the critic cannot help but regard his work as an end in itself, for in reacting to art he is expressing his own ideas, elaborating his own meanings and in fact projecting a vision of life, even if only in an indirect and piecemeal fashion, by actively absorbing and pronouncing upon the visions of the artists that engage him? It is nevertheless true that in the economy of literature as a whole criticism is, objectively speaking, seldom an end in itself but mostly a means toward an end. What that ultimate end is we can define, after acknowledging its immediate ends of elucidating and evaluating works of art, under the double aspect of assimilation and mediation. To elucidate and evaluate a work of art is to assimilate it, and assimilation is in essence an act of mediating— mediating between art and the individual artist, between tradition and novelty, between the parts and the whole, and, in the long run, between art and life. This is culturally a function of the highest value, an indispensable one in fact; but it is in the main a function of cultural service and utility. Criticism exhausts itself in accomplishing it, which explains why it has so low a survival value in comparison with other genres of writing. It would seem as if in the very act of using criticism as liberally as we do we make and unmake it.

3

I would like to propose a distinction between types of criticism, a distinction that has little to do with the arid issues of methodology but is centered rather on the quality and import of the critic's interest in the literary process. In my view, there are chiefly two approaches that critics follow, one being prospective and the other retrospective. An excellent though somewhat one-sided example of the prospective attitude is Wordsworth's famous *Preface*. It is an attitude that asserts itself whenever the critic conceives of literature as something actual and alive in his own time and relates himself to it by trying to affect its course of development here and now. Both Eliot and Pound had this approach in mind when they first made their influence felt, as when Pound said that criticism is at its best when it is "definitely shot at new creation, at a reinvigoration of writing." In *The Sacred Wood* Eliot put it that "the important critic is the person who is absorbed in the present problems of art, and who wishes to bring the forces of the past to bear upon the solution of these problems." What is indispensable, he argued in another essay in the same volume, is "a creative interest, a focus upon the immediate future"; and

it was exactly that focus, of course, adjusted with beautiful cal-
culation, that made for the extraordinary cogency of Eliot's
reassessment of the order of English poetry.

This quality of absorption in the present problems of literary
art, this sense of it as continuous and open to the incursions of
the sensibility in its dynamic changes and responses to new
experience, is missing in the retrospective critic, who tends to
take literature as something given once and for all, secure in
its pastness and unopen toward the future. Retrospective criticism may be good or bad of its kind, it may be extremely useful
or nearly useless, but it is always marked by taking for granted
that what matters are not the potentialities of literature but its
norms. This type of criticism may be written by professors, by
free-lance critics, or by literary journalists; it is the lack of a
creative and intentional concern that makes it retrospective.
Nor is it in the least a question of the critic's subject matter.
Prospective criticism, though preoccupied with present problems, is hardly limited to contemporary literature. It may deal
with the literature of the past or of the present or both. But
in dealing with the past it does so with a certain intention—
so well illustrated, for instance, in Eliot's essays on the Elizabethan dramatists and seventeenth-century poetry—the intention plainly being that of mobilizing the masterpieces of the
past as a means of reactivating the creative imagination of its
own time. Both Coleridge and Arnold shared this particular
intention, if not in all then surely in a good part of their work.
It is this relation to the past that makes the literary heritage
come alive for us, whereas the retrospective critic makes it
available to us as an object of study, of intense professional
curiosity or antiquarian pleasure, but seldom as a living
experience.

Of present-day criticism one might say many things but
scarcely that its impact is of a prospective character. In the work
of its finer representatives this criticism displays many assets,
such as erudition, eloquence, virtuosity in the selecting and
presenting of literary evidence, and intellectual brilliance; but
it is quite clear that it is incapable of serving even in part as

the motive power of new creation. It is much too self-contained and safely adjusted to its limited role to undertake the commitments that a programmatic approach to writing exacts from its partisans. As for "the forces of the past" invoked by Eliot, criticism is now marvelously aware of those forces and has no end of traffic with them, though by and large this is a one-way traffic that gets us past rather than into the present problems of art. To be sure, a plea might be entered in defence of contemporary criticism on the ground that, in the absence of a powerful new impulse among creative writers, it can be hardly expected to strike out on its own to perform a function which the history of literature shows to be more naturally and confidently performed in periods witnessing a renewal of imaginative energy and the emergence of insurgent tendencies in the national culture. It should be recalled, too, that the criticism of the generation of Eliot and Pound that might be described as "definitely shot at new creation" was produced not apart from but in conjunction with its literary practice, the sensibility and techniques of which needed, first, to be defined with precision and then justified in the light both of the rediscovery of tradition and of the revolt against it.

But there is another type of prospective criticism, in its way quite as valuable, I think, as that aimed at the immediate reinvigoration of writing, to which contemporary critics might profitably address themselves. This is the type of which Matthew Arnold gave classic definition in his essay "The Function of Criticism at the Present Time." In that essay Arnold was of course mainly concerned with the relationship between the critical and the creative power, and in particular with the operative meaning of that relationship in uncreative periods; and it is by reason of that emphasis that the argument of Arnold's celebrated essay seems to me to bear closely upon our situation. In his view, literary talent mostly manifests itself not in the unfolding of new ideas, not in "synthesis and exposition" but in "analysis and discovery," its great faculty being that of becoming "happily inspired by a certain intellectual and spiritual atmosphere, by a certain order of ideas, when it finds itself in them." Arnold had a far broader and more flexible notion of the relevance of ideas to the imaginative life than that prevailing in our literary world, where ideas are commonly assumed to exert a devitalizing influence on creative effort. Arnold, on the other hand, perceived that ideas, in his richly suggestive and socially viable sense of the term, composed the very element with which "the creative power works," and he held it as certain that in modern literature especially no display of the creative power in disengagement from that element could prove to be "important or fruitful." The fine concreteness of his historical insight is shown in this last observation, no less than in his further observation that the ideas literature works with cannot be those that are accessible at any time but only those that are "current at the time," that is to say, only those which historical development has made actually and directly available to the imagination. Now the creative power, for its effective exercise, must have the requisite atmosphere, it must dispose of itself amidst an order of fructifying ideas. But this atmosphere and order are not within its control. "This is why the great epochs in literature are so rare . . . for the creation of a masterwork two powers must concur, the power of the man and the power of the moment, and the man is not enough without the moment." It is that "moment" that the applied vigor of criticism can help to bring about through its own means of prefigurement and preparation, since, potentially at least, its aptitudes are scarcely so meager as not to be able to contribute to the making of an intellectual situation of which the creative power can avail itself.

That this account of the interaction that sometimes occurs between the critical and creative faculties is substantially correct can be demonstrated from numerous examples from literary history. It is unnecessary to go far afield into foreign literatures to illustrate this interaction. Consider, for instance, the ferment of ideas that occurred in this country in the 1830's and '40's, a ferment which can only partially be identified with Transcendentalism and the inner meaning of which is now lost on us. The point is that it is this ferment of ideas which instigated changes in the literary consciousness, without which such masterworks as *The Scarlet Letter, Moby Dick,* and *Leaves of Grass* might conceivably never have been written. Or consider the seminal influence in this century, again in Arnold's sense of establishing a new atmosphere and a new intellectual situation, of critics like Mencken, the early Van Wyck Brooks, Randolph Bourne on the one hand and the group of poetry-critics taking their cue from Eliot and Pound on the other. However much those critics differed among themselves, they were alike in the immense stimulus they provided to the national literature by striking boldly, openly, and with exhilarating success, at the forces that had long inhibited its growth.

The type of prospective criticism of which Arnold speaks in his essay is patently criticism only in the broadest sense of the term. Being educative and preparative in intent, it is as much a criticism of the larger context of literature as of its specific texts. Still, that is no reason for belittling it; we misunderstand the critical task if we conceive of it as unvarying from age to age; the changing needs of literature are the goad of criticism. In this period we have gone so far in specificity and formalistic detachment as to neglect the wider and more vital interests of American writing. The impulse that animated this writing in the first half of the century is apparently exhausted. A fresh impulse can arise only from a new quickening of thought reaching out from the life within literature toward the greater life by which it is encompassed on all sides.

THE BEGINNING WRITER IN
THE UNIVERSITY

~~~~~~~~~

by Malcolm Cowley

"How can I become a professional writer?" is a question I have been asked in various fashions by persons of all ages from under eighteen to—in a recent case—over eighty, and I never know how to answer those of any age. Of course I might say to some, if I knew them better, "You'd be wise to give up the idea. It's too late now to make up for the years when you should have been reading everything and writing for practice." To others I might say, also knowing them better, "You don't really want to write, which is the worst sort of drudgery. You have a romantic dream of being a writer. You want to have inspirations, then put them on paper in a sort of prolonged and painless trance, like having a baby under anesthetic, then stand around at cocktail parties answering questions about your last book, so wittily but modestly too, between deep puffs at your pipe. Why not dream of being a movie actor instead?"

To still others I might say, "You seem to have talent, but I suspect you of having a beautiful soul. Let me warn you that the competition is brutal and that you may be too delicate to survive in a field where the more one tries to be sensitive in one's work, the more one has to be tough with oneself." And again I might say, for example to college students who were not only talented but also appeared to have a more dogged ambition, "Write a great deal and get it published." That is always sound advice, but if they asked another question, "How can I learn to make my writing good enough to be published?" once again I should be doubtful how to answer

them. Today there is no generally available form of apprenticeship, no clearly marked path for qualified beginners that will
lead them into the writing profession.

That wasn't always the case in American writing. We can
see in retrospect that during the nineteenth century there
were two such paths, each of them followed by many young
men with literary ambitions. I have mentioned these paths
before, in a book called *The Literary Situation,* but I make
no apology for repeating myself, because the facts are necessary
as a background for what I want to say. One of the paths led
through a divinity school, usually Harvard, and later through
the pastorate of a small church, most often Unitarian. The
young minister would write for chuch magazines, then for
general magazines or book publishers, and finally he would
resign his pastorate. Writers trained as clergymen had the great
advantage of a flowing style, acquired in the pulpit; for most
of them the words came easily. They had the disadvantage that
the style was intended to impress a congregation, instead of
being directed to the hearts and minds of individuals.

The other path appears to have held more promise for writers,
not as moral teachers. It was the one that started in a printing
shop, usually in the composing room of a weekly newspaper.
After leaving school at fourteen or fifteen, the apprentice man
of letters was employed there as a copy boy or printer's devil;
then he would be taught how to read proof and how to set
type by hand. It was the most practical sort of training, for at
worst or least the apprentice would learn the rules of grammar,
punctuation, and spelling—which are becoming an esoteric
form of knowledge—and at best he would learn another lesson
as well. By handling a type-metal alphabet, he would learn that
words have body and weight as well as sound; he would acquire
an almost tactile sense of language; and he would also learn
that big words and oratorical turns of phrase wasted his time,
like that of readers.

The first truly effective American writer, Benjamin Franklin,
was a printer, just as the second, Jonathan Edwards, was a
clergyman. In the nineteenth century the writers who followed

Ben Franklin's path were, among others, Whitman, Howells, Bret Harte, Mark Twain, and Lafcadio Hearn, all of whom set type at some stage in their early careers and each of whom learned to write fluent and accurate English. After setting type for a newspaper, they each wrote stories for it. The best of their stories were reprinted so widely that magazine editors began asking for their work, then book publishers, and they were launched on their literary careers—sometimes without quite knowing how it had happened.

After 1890 most of the newspaper composing rooms were unionized and no longer offered casual employment to school-boys serving their literary apprenticeships. The new path to recognition led through the city room of a big-town newspaper, where the miserably underpaid staff kept changing and there were always jobs for ambitious young men. If they survived the first few years—as not all of them did in those hard-drinking days—young writers learned to get their facts in proper sequence and learned a great deal about the tough underbelly of American life. On the other hand, most of them never acquired the devout feeling for words that was shown by earlier writers who had worked in printing shops. Dreiser, Mencken, Huneker, Harold Frederic, Stephen Crane, Jack Reed, and David Graham Phillips—in fact most of the new writers who appeared between 1890 and 1915—got their start as cub reporters.

Today the situation has changed again. Newspaper work has ceased to be a poorly paid apprenticeship for other professions, including authorship, and has become a rewarding career in itself. On-the-job training for writers is something that still exists in a few places, but the places are hard to find. Most of the beginners go to college, and many of them continue into graduate schools, where they are exposed to the best education this country has ever offered. Unfortunately, if they still want to be writers, not critics or teachers, it isn't always or often the best education for the special careers they have in mind.

This general tendency in the field of writing—I mean the decline of apprenticeship, with our educational system coming forward to supply the professional training on all levels no longer provided by masters and employers—is one that extends into all fields of American life. Many of our high schools are being transformed into trade schools, offering a maximum of shop practice with only a seasoning dash of book learning. The demand for professional training has forced our universities to expand far beyond the original four faculties of theology, law, medicine, and the liberal arts. Engineeering first, then agriculture, forestry, schoolteaching, nursing, advertising, selling, management of all types, horticulture, household economics, getting married, having babies: almost every human activity has become a subject for university instruction, often at the postgraduate level. For the artistic and literary professions, there are many famous schools or departments of architecture, journalism, music, design in all its branches, and the drama. A similar development is taking place in the field of writing, but here the professional training has neither been carried so far nor organized in such a systematic manner as in other fields. Indeed, the popularity of courses in advanced writing is a fairly recent development.

So far as I have been able to learn, the first writing course for students who seriously planned to become men of letters was given at Harvard in the 1890's by Lewis E. Gates. To judge by his students, who included a number of brilliant poets and novelists, he must have been a gifted teacher. Frank Norris' first novel, *Vandover and the Brute*, was one of those written in Gates's course. A few years later the same sort of instruction was being given at Michigan by Fred Newton Scott, who was Avery Hopwood's admired professor and thus was indirectly the cause of these awards and this lecture.

When Gates died in 1903, his place at Harvard was taken by two other famous teachers: the scholarly Dean Briggs, whose deeply wrinkled face bore a look of sympathy and saintliness, and C. T. Copeland—"Copey," as everybody called him—who was more of an actor than a saint or scholar, but who had a keen eye for details and an ear that quickly distinguished good from awkward prose. At conferences he used to sit back in his armchair like a pale-bronze Buddha and listen while we read our themes aloud; then he would dictate a comment for us to write. I remember two of these. Once when I had described the swirling dust in a Pittsburgh street he asked, "Don't you remember the smell of dried horse dung? Why didn't you put that in?" And once when I read him a sententious editorial written for the *Harvard Advocate,* in which one wondered how the country knew who . . . , he shook his bald head, with a shifting highlight on it from the afternoon sun, and groaned, "Malcolm, when are you going to stop using those knew-whoings and one-wonderings?" I stopped that afternoon.

In the first two decades of this century, Harvard was a seed-bed and plant nursery of American authorship. Almost all the writers who were there in any of the years from 1905 to 1920 took either Copey's course or Dean Briggs's course, or both of them. The only exceptions were the thirteen dramatic writers—Baker's Dozen—admitted each year to George Pierce Baker's English 47 Workshop. In that period when all Americans worshiped success, and especially early success, an event of the year 1907 gave a special prestige to the 47 Workshop, as if it had been sprinkled with gold dust, some of which rubbed off on the other advanced writing courses. The event was the long Broadway run of Edward Sheldon's play, *Salvation Nell,* which had been written in English 47 while Sheldon was still an undergraduate. Later Eugene O'Neill was a still more famous product of the course.

In 1925 Baker moved his 47 Workshop to Yale, where a school of the drama was built around it. In 1931 the University of Michigan, which had retained a lively interest in writing courses, was enabled to broaden its program and offer these prizes as a result of the Hopwood bequest. Soon other universities were trying to attract young writers. Courses in advanced or, as it is usually miscalled, creative writing are now being offered by institutions all over the country, and there are good ones at some of the smaller colleges, like Kenyon, for example. At Stanford the writing program has been given its own endowment. At Iowa there is a postgraduate school of writing that confers a master's degree, with the student submitting a novel or a book of poems as his magisterial theis.

Most of the present courses everywhere are conducted by able and devoted teachers. Most of the students—of course not all of them—are willing to work seriously and aren't taking the courses just for credit. Many of the former students have made names for themselves, as one can see by reading a list of the former Hopwood Awards. If the courses accomplish less than the teachers hope for them, perhaps that results from a misconception of what they might properly accomplish.

Sometimes the misconception is embodied in the name of the course: Creative Writing, Creating the Novel, Creating the Short Story, or even Creating the Fifteen-Minute Script. I doubt that any instructor, however earnest or inspired, can teach any group of students, however talented, to create anything whatever. He cannot give them experience of the world, or a desire to communicate the experience, or do more for their power of invention than merely to encourage it, if the power already exists. What he can properly teach the students, or expose them to the opportunity of learning, are the rules and practices to be deduced from other people's writing, the standards of the writing profession, and the resources of language as a medium. He cannot teach the *art* of writing, but that in itself is a complicated study and most writers never learn enough of it.

Partly because of a false emphasis on the art rather than the craft, some writing programs become suffused with an atmosphere of artiness, of waiting for inspirations that don't always come—and when they do come, the student has not enough of the craft to embody them in the necessary words. Other teachers, trying to be more realistic, avoid this emphasis and like to say that they could never teach their students how to write—"But at least," they add, "we can teach them how to read." So the so-called workshop in creative writing is transformed into an exercise in critical analysis, very useful to most students, but not necessarily serving as a prologue or apprenticeship to their own work. Sometimes it has the opposite effect of developing their critical sense to the point where they can't write at all, or can write nothing but explications for the literary quarterlies.

I think there is another kind of writing program that might be offered. In a completely dogmatic and rather impractical fashion, with no attention to administrative problems and chiefly as a basis for discussion, I should like to suggest what such a program might be.

Its purpose would be to teach the skills that are needed by every professional writer. It would be concerned with working habits, with problems of structure and style, and with methods that writers in the past have found for solving them—not forgetting that new writers might try to find new methods, better suited to their personalities. In other words, the program would not be creational or expressional or inspirational or analytical or therapeutic, but, I hope in the best sense of the word, professional—like the best of the programs now being offered in architecture, the drama, and musical composition.

It would be open to juniors and seniors, with an optional third year for graduate students. For juniors and seniors it would require at least as many hours of credit as the present honors program in English literature. In the postgraduate year it would be designed to occupy the whole, or almost the whole, of the student's time. There would be no second postgraduate year, because the student should then be ready for practical experience in writing. There is one thing he should never be encouraged to do, that is, to travel from university to university, taking more and more writing courses, supporting himself with fellowships, and never getting his work published—until at last, like a student I used to know, he gets married and accepts a post at some teachers' college in the alkali belt as an instructor in creative writing.

The instructors in the program I have in mind would be men with a passion for teaching younger men and women how to write, and with the hope that they will some day find and help to train a writer of genius to justify their teaching. Whether they should be professional writers themselves is a question that won't ever be settled. Many or most of the famous instructors today are writers who manage to combine their professional careers with college instruction. I might mention among others Archibald MacLeish and Albert Guérard, Jr., at Harvard; Robert Penn Warren, until recently at Yale; R. P. Blackmur at Princeton, John Crowe Ransom at Kenyon, Allen Tate at Minnesota, Karl Shapiro at Nebraska, Hudson Strode at Alabama, Mark Schorer and George R. Stewart at California, Wallace Stegner at Stanford, and Allan Seager and John Frederick Muehl at this university. All these men have published several books, and whatever they tell their students has the weight of practical experience behind it.

On the other hand, most of the famous instructors of the past were not professional writers, and here I am thinking of men like Gates, Copeland, Briggs, Baker, Fred Newton Scott, and R. W. Cowden. The greatest writing teacher of our age was not a writer, or connected with any university, but he had a passion for good writing and the passion was communicated to others. He was a publisher's editor, the late Maxwell E. Perkins, who was the friend of Hemingway and Fitzgerald, the spiritual father of Thomas Wolfe, and the adviser of many capable if less distinguished authors. It should be noted, and not incidentally, that Perkins and the older instructors I have mentioned could write very well when they were called upon to write or forced themselves to do so. That ability should be required of every instructor in a writing program. There are many English professors, highly respected in the academic world, who should be disqualified as teachers of writing by the first paragraph, even the first sentence, of any critical study they have contributed to the *PMLA Quarterly*.

A requirement for students in the program is that they should have distinguished themselves in whatever writing courses they may have taken during their first two years of college work. They need not have distinguished themselves in other courses, because the sad fact is that future novelists and dramatists, unlike future critics and some poets, aren't always the brightest students in courses outside their own field. Every student in the program should prove himself capable of writing clear sentences and well-constructed paragraphs. One reason for such a requirement is that instructors shouldn't have to bother with these fundamentals, but there is the additional reason that future men of letters are more likely to reveal themselves by their passion for getting the words right than by their wealth of material. Eventually they will be judged by what they say, but their early promise depends more on how they say it.

I should hope that the program would be difficult enough to frighten away the mere yearners and tender spirits and seekers for help in unfolding their precious personalities. It is the difficult programs that attract the best students—and if the program I have in mind proved difficult enough and fruitful enough, it might attract good students from all parts of the country.

It would include three or four subjects that are not usually taught in universities, even the largest. For example, it might begin with what might be called—even if we don't like the word—an indoctrination course on the history of the writing profession. Entirely too much attention is being paid to the faults and delinquencies of famous writers, with the result that people have formed a false picture of the profession as a refuge for the weak, the abnormal, the self-indulgent, and the self-destructive. Not only the public but young writers too are being encouraged to forget that writing is a profession with its own difficult standards of conduct, with its high virtues and with sins like dishonesty and self-deception that are regarded as sins against the Holy Ghost. Writing has its saints and heroes—like Keats and Flaubert, who is sometimes a dangerous model; like Trollope as antidote to Flaubert; like Tolstoy, James, Conrad, and Thomas Mann—and their lives might be studied as models of courage for the new generation.

There would also be a course in the creative process, or simply in the mechanics of finding a subject, developing it in words, and putting the words on paper. The course would include such topics as how to observe a scene, how to remember it, how to visualize, how to meditate on a subject, in the manner of Hawthorne and Henry James, how to write first drafts, and finally how to revise what one has written. But there would be other topics too: how to take notes or not to take them, how to make outlines and scenarios, when to write and where, and how long every day. Most of these questions have a different practical answer for each writer, and the answers have to be found by experiment. Accordingly there might be such practical exercises as writing at different times of the day (including midnight and six o'clock in the morning), writing alone, writing in the company of friends, and writing in a room full of strangers. Every student should practice different methods of putting words on paper—with pen or pencil, with a typewriter, and by dictation—so as to learn the essential lesson that writing goes on in the head and that putting down the words is merely a process of transcription.

Again there might be a course in translation from a foreign language, simply because translation is a most effective means of learning the spirit and resources of one's own language. There is no better way of acquiring a prose style, except possibly the writing of verse. Such a course should be given in the English Department, or better in the writing program, by an instructor familiar with three or more foreign languages, though each of the students would have to know only one of them. The emphasis of the course would not be on an accurate rendering of the original, though a reasonable degree of fidelity would be expected, but rather on the value of the translation as English prose.

The core of the writing program would consist of four courses, each lasting a semester, and all required of undergraduates who specialize in the field. They would be courses in writing stories, in writing short plays, in writing nonfiction, and in writing verse. I say "verse" because it would be unreasonable to expect students with a primary talent for fictional or nonfictional prose to produce anything that might properly be called poetry. But there is no reason why they shouldn't learn to write verse, according to the traditional rules of English prosody, or why they shouldn't be called upon to produce, for example, Elizabethan blank verse, Spenserian stanzas, rhymed quatrains in iambic pentameter, eighteenth-century heroic couplets, and Petrarchan sonnets. Scott Fitzgerald said in a letter to his daughter, who wanted to write, "The only thing that will help you is poetry, which is the most concentrated form of style." And in another letter he said, "I don't think anyone can write succinct prose unless they have at least tried and failed to write a good iambic pentameter sonnet."

I think the course in writing verse would come first among the four writing courses, because, in the history of literature, verse comes before prose. Then would come writing plays, to get an ear for dialogue and a sense of construction; writing stories, a practice that includes the other skills; and writing non-fiction, which comes last because good nonfiction involves the use of fictional techniques. In all the courses there would be a similar emphasis, not on self-expression, but on the methods and conventions of the given medium. The student would learn the rules before breaking them, so as not to break them through awkwardness or inadvertence. Most of the exercises would be on assigned topics or problems. Only in the postgraduate year would the student go to work on a longer project of his own choosing: a novel, a collection of stories, a full-length play, or a book of essays or poems.

I am not thinking here of the future critics, who would require a different sort of preparation, more in the conventional field of English and foreign literature. Still, they might be required to take at least two of the writing courses, and perhaps all four of them, so as to gain some first-hand knowledge of the problems faced by other writers. A good deal of our present-day criticism has gone up in the air, as if in an untethered balloon. It is impressive and ingenious, but it doesn't always make sense to those who have undergone the drudgery of writing a novel or a play in verse. Taking courses like those I suggest might give our critics a sharper sense of reality.

As for courses outside the writing field that students in the writing program might take as undergraduates, there would be more than a little individual choice and diversity. Writers are primarily men of words, and it is not a bad idea for the apprentice writer to learn as many words or signs in as many languages as possible—not only French, German, or Spanish and Latin, but the special language of the sciences, or philosophy, or mathematics—if he has any talent in that direction—and perhaps even the barbarous language of sociology. Writers have to deal with human beings in social groups, and it is a good idea for the apprentice writer to learn something about history, psychology, anthropology, mythology, and human relations. There should be a close cooperation, with exchange of courses, between the writing program and the departments of speech and journalism. Perhaps it is better for the writing student to know a little about many fields outside his own than to learn a great deal about one field. In particular I think it is dangerous for him to specialize—as many young writers now do—in contemporary literature and in the close analysis of texts. He should read a great deal of contemporary literature, in college and afterward, but he should read it for himself, to find what he really thinks about it and not what he is supposed to think.

Remember that I am speaking at this point about students who want to become professional writers, not about those who want to become teachers or merely wish to acquire a general education. Every professional writer is at least a double personality: he is at the same time a compulsive speaker, at least under his voice, and a severe listener to his own speech; a creature of instinct or emotion and a cold reasoner; a creator—to use the proud word—and a critic. In great writers these two sides of the literary personality are both developed to the utmost possible degree. In little writers and failed writers they are out of balance—usually because the critical side is too weak, but sometimes for the opposite reason, because it has developed too far and too fast. The sort of training that is best for a future critic or teacher—the sort now given in our best universities—is often dangerous for an apprentice writer. If he spends too much time on the close analysis of texts, especially modern texts, the critical side of him ceases to be a listener, making its critical comments in an undertone; the voice of the critic becomes louder, firmer, more admonitory, and perhaps the other voice, that of instinct or emotion, may be frightened back into the depths of the mind.

There is a traditional way of teaching advanced writing courses, one that goes back to Gates's course at Harvard in the 1890's. The class is small, usually consisting of from ten to fifteen students. It meets once a week for a two-hour session, and sometimes there is a second meeting as well. At each meeting one of the students reads his latest story—or a short play, or a chapter from the novel he may be working on—then the other students make their comments and perhaps offer suggestions for improving his work. In addition the instructor has a conference with each of the students, usually once every two weeks.

I have met writing instructors, including two or three very good ones, who prefer not to meet their students as a group and who work with them only in the private conferences. These instructors say that class meetings lead to an unhealthy sort of rivalry. They say that a student who reads his work in class is likely to become painfully self-conscious. They also say that the other students are sometimes too harsh in their comments, having adopted this means of asserting their own superiority, and at other times are entirely too gentle, because they will have to read in their turns and because they hope to be treated with equal kindness.

In spite of these valid observations and the difficulties they reveal, I believe that the traditional method of teaching advanced writing courses is still the best—though always with the the proviso that each writing instructor must find his own most effective way. It would seem to me, however, that the class meetings are almost as necessary as the private conferences, and that a combination of the two is best for the instructor because it ends by saving his time. Most of the advice he has to offer can be utilized by all his students and might as well be addressed to them as a group. Then, in the private conferences, he can deal with finer points of structure and style. But class meetings are desirable for the students too, because they can learn at least as much from one another as from the instructor, and sometimes they learn much more. Reading their work aloud teaches them to judge its effect on an audience. They learn whether the points they tried to make are being understood, and whether their own words are awkward to pronounce. The test of good prose is reading it aloud.

As for the competitive spirit that develops when each of the students waits for his work to be jeered at or praised, it can lead to a morbid sort of jealousy, but it can also lead to harder work and better craftsmanship. There is no reason to make a secret of the fact that writing is a highly competitive profession, and that every writer is jealous in some degree of every other writer whom he suspects of being more facile or inventive or held in higher esteem than himself. But the literary mind has another aspect too, and writers as a group are more willing to help one another and quicker to recognize talent than members of most other professions, feeling as they do that sacrifices are owed to their art. Beginners in the profession might as well be exposed to this mixture of jealousy and generosity at a very early stage in their careers, so as to inure themselves to praise and blame, like Indian boys learning to undergo cold and hunger. Then the young writers may be better prepared for the ordeal of having their first books treated as masterpieces, or dismissed in a few contemptuous words, or simply overlooked.

The spirit of competition will always appear in a writing class, but the spirit of cooperation might well be encouraged. One way to encourage it is to have the class, or members of the class, embark on some common undertaking. The project method has been applied with great success in schools of architecture, where teams of students are formed in the graduating class and each team is given some big architectural problem to solve. It has been applied with success in schools or departments of journalism, where students collaborate in pro-

ducing a sort of laboratory newspaper. Since the days when
George Pierce Baker was teaching at Harvard, it has also been
applied in schools of the drama, where many students work
together on the production of a play that one of them wrote
and all of them criticized. There is no reason why a similar
method might not be utilized in writing programs.

Any one of a number of common projects might be undertaken by an advanced writing class, or by chosen members of
the class. For example, the project might be the preparation of
a book-length manuscript containing the best stories produced
in the class, or the best plays or poems. If there were funds available for the purpose and if the manuscript was good enough, it
might be published. At Stanford the best stories from the top
writing class are chosen each year by vote of the class itself
and are issued as a book by the Stanford University Press. That
gives the class pride in itself as a group and a definite goal toward which to work.

A project for writing students who want to become teachers
or critics is to prepare a collection of critical essays on a given
subject. I tried that experiment at the University of Washington some years ago, in a graduate seminar. The task assigned
to the class was to write a book on contemporary American literature, in which each student would deal with a particular
author. There happened to be some gifted students in the
class of sixteen, and nine or ten of the long essays deserved
and were ready to be published. The university press was
willing to undertake the book if it could be put into shape.
Unfortunately not all the students were on the same level of
achievement, and two or three of the least capable were dealing
with authors who couldn't be omitted. Even so we could have
brought the whole book up to publication level if we had had a
few more weeks to work on it instead of a single academic
quarter.

A less ambitious project for a writing class—and less expensive for the university than publishing a bound book with a
problematical sale—is for the class to issue, during the year, two
or three numbers of a magazine containing the best work of

its members in all fields. The class would not only write the magazine but would act as a board of editors to select material and suggest desirable revisions; and members of the class would be assigned to act as copyreaders and proofreaders. If funds were not available to print the magazine from type, the manuscripts could be copied on an electric typewriter and mimeographed or multigraphed or printed by the offset method; by now there are many inexpensive methods of reproducing written words. The magazine wouldn't be sold, so as not to compete with independent periodicals, including those issued by undergraduates, but it might be distributed free to bigger magazines and publishing houses. Not only would it offer practical experience to students in a writing program, but it would serve as a showcase for their work and perhaps as a first step toward wider publication.

And what would be the end result of such a program, for students who took part in it?

The directors of the program could not promise to make them great writers or popular writers. For that they would need inborn or inbred qualities that no course of professional training could supply. They would have to possess what Thomas Wolfe called "the foremost quality of the artist, without which he is lost: the ability to get out of his own life the power to live and work by, to derive from his own experience— as a fruit of all his seeing, feeling, living, joy and bitter anguish—the palpable and living substance of his art." Beyond that they would have to possess obstinate patience and energy, combined with more than the usual degree of critical judgment. But if they did possess this rare combination of talents—a combination that is unlikely to reveal itself at an early age—the talents would not be wasted, as they often are today, for want of practice and for ignorance of the fundamental writing skills.

For others in the program who proved to have critical judgment but lacked the sort of obstinate energy that good writers require, another prospect might be opened. As crowded as the writing profession seems to be at certain levels, there are hundreds and thousands of modest but necessary and sometimes remunerative places in the profession that are not being properly filled for want of younger men and women with the necessary training. I am thinking of places like those of copy editors, story editors, scenario and script writers, feature writers, business and technical writers, translators, revisers of manuscripts, collaborators (sometimes known as ghosts), play doctors, and book reviewers—a whole collection of honest literary trades that are now being practiced either cynically, for shudders and laughs, or else, in many cases, with a painful degree of ignorance and ineptitude. They should be practiced with competence and integrity, not only for the sake of the literary profession and the public, but also for the sake of literature as an art—because high standards in all the literary crafts are the foundation from which great works can rise, like towers against the sky.

THE SILENCES OF POETRY

by John Ciardi

A poem, by the very fact of its existence in time rather than in space, has *duration* and *pace*. Since it does not move throughout at exactly the same pace (there must be some acceleration or impedance, no matter how slight), the poem must also have *change of pace;* one part moves more rapidly or more slowly than another. All such changes of pace, it must be noted, are relative to one another: an anapest introduced into an iambic line accelerates that part of the line; an anapest in an anapestic line sustains the already established pace, but does not accelerate it. All the rhythms of poetry achieve their effect by the way they play against one another. They exist in countermotion.

Similarly, *all* the elements of a poem are engaged in a series of countermotions. Meter and rhythm are only two of the elements that may be involved. Diction, imagery, rhyme, line length, vowel quantities, consonant sequences, and grammatical structure are some of the other principal elements. From these elements the poem builds complexes of poetic structures, each related to all the others. The motion of these poetic structures, each against the others, is what ultimately determines the poem's performance. One simple rule seems to apply to the play of all such countermotions: *Whenever in the course of a poem the poet changes either his tone or his attitude, some change will occur in the handling of the technical elements.* That change in the technical handling of the poem may be slight or it may be marked, but some change must occur. Conversely, any change in the handling of the technical elements in the course of the poem will indicate that a change has taken place in the author's tone or attitude. Attitude, in Robert Frost's phrase, may be taken to signify "the way the poet takes his subject"; tone, "the way he takes himself."

The following little poem ("The Span of Life," by Robert Frost) will serve as a convenient first illustration:

> The old dog barks backward without getting up.
> I can remember when he was a pup.

Note that neither line is a poem by itself. It is not a poem to say "The old dog barks backward without getting up." That much is only a statement. Nor is it a poem to say "I can remember when he was a pup." That much is only a comment. Yet it is clear that a poem does happen when the two lines are said one after the other. It must follow that the poem exists in the countermotion of the two lines, in the way the second line (in this case the comment) makes something of what has been established in the first line (in this case the statement). Nor do the two lines simply run together; there is some point of balance between the end of the first line and the beginning of the second, a pause, a meditative silence like a rest in music. The poem enters that pause with one attitude (in this case relatively detached specific observation of the old dog) and after a moment of meditation it comes out of the pause with a different attitude (in this case a double change involving, first, a fonder, a sadder, a more general recollection of the dog, and, second, a metaphoric implication, as reinforced by the title, that the comment is not only about the old dog but about all of life).

For convenience such points of balance (and silence) may be called fulcrums and may be indicated by the symbol <, thus:

> The old dog barks backward without getting up.
>
>   <
> I can remember when he was a pup.

Such countermotion is inseparable from "what the poem is" and "what the poem means"; it is in fact *"how* the poem means." In briefest form, *a poem is one part against another across a silence.* To understand this characteristic of the poem is to understand the theory of poetic form. To be able to respond to it in a poem is to understand the practice of poetry.[1]

The Frost poem is as simple an example of poetic countermotion as one may well find. The following poem ("O Western Wind") will illustrate the same sort of countermotion with rather more marked changes occurring across the fulcrum. The poem is

[1] I claimed earlier that every shift in tone or attitude is accompanied by some shift in the handling of the technical elements. That shift is relatively difficult to establish in so brief a poem since it involves the metrical differences between two lines, each of which is unusual. The norm is, of course, anapestic, and one will do well to note at least some of the ways in which these lines vary in their play against that norm. The first line may be scanned:

The old dog / barks back / ward wi thout / ge tting up.

Yet certainly there is good reason for wishing to distribute the stress of the first foot over both "old" and "dog," thus:

The old dog / barks back / ward wi thout / ge tting up.

The fact that one must pause after saying "old" in order to form the "d" sound of dog, tends to force a heavy stress on both words. The similarity of the vowels tends to make the words equal. And the repetition of "b" and "k" sounds around a similar (not identical) vowel sound in "barks back" once more heightens the pattern. Thus one is tempted to cluster four heavy accents on "old dog barks back."

The second line, on the other hand, has only one complication and that in the first (monosyllabic) foot. After the first foot the line progresses to the close in flawless anapests (the norm):

I / can re mem / ber when he / was a pup.

One will do well to note the unusually heavy accent at the beginning of the second line (in this case a monosyllabic foot). Though it is not an invariable rule, there is a strong tendency in English and American poetry for the line after a fulcrum to begin with an unusually heavy stress, a monosyllabic foot, a spondee, a reversed foot, or some combination of these accents that produces a cluster of heavy stresses. The line can, of course, be scanned with the first two feet rendered as trochee and iamb, but it certainly seems wiser to emphasize the dominant anapestic pattern. Either rendering will indicate almost the same voice emphases.

one of the most memorable of the anonymous ballad snatches
surviving from the early sixteenth century or perhaps earlier.
Like most folk balladry, it survives in variant forms. The following is a modernized version.

> O Western wind, when wilt thou blow
>   That the small rain down may rain?
>   <
> Christ, that my love were in my arms,
>   And I in my bed again.

As indicated by the fulcrum, the poem, like "The Span of
Life," consists of two parts. The first two lines are a cry of
anguish to the western wind (in England, the wind of Spring).
The lament issues without any statement of cause for the
speaker's anguish. The second two lines snap off that generalized lament and utter an angry and specific protest. The poet's
tone has undergone an emphatic change.

As in "The Span of Life," one may note at once that neither
of the halves is a poem. Whatever is being experienced is not
complete in either the first two or the last two lines, but
achieves its completion only in their countermotion across the
silence of the fulcrum. Now if one will study the differences
in technical handling on either side of the fulcrum, and if he
will then relate them to the emotional force of the poem, he
will be approaching the poem as its own performance, as its own
act of itself, without resort to the confusion by paraphrase.

For though paraphrase may be useful in helping to explain a
specific difficulty in the phrasing of a poem, it is unfailingly
a destructive method of discussion if one permits the illusion
that the paraphrase is more than a momentary crutch, or that
it is in any sense the poem itself. No poem "means" anything
that any paraphrase is capable of saying. For, as noted, the
poem exists in time and it exists in balance and countermotion
across a silence. That timing and that counterthrust are inseparable from the emotional force of the poem, and it is exactly
that timing and counterthrust that paraphrase cannot repro-

duce. The question to put to the poem is not "What does it mean?" but "How does it mean?" "What does it mean?" inevitably invites paraphrase and inevitably leads away from the poem. "How does it mean?" is best asked by absorbing the poetic structure as a poetic structure, i.e., as a countermotion across a silence, and thus leads the analysis to the poem itself.

In "O Western Wind" the two most notable differences between the lines before and after the fulcrum are (1) the pace, as determined by the metrics, by the consonant-vowel sequences, and by the rhetorical structure; and (2) the diction, which changes from formal-hortatory in the first two lines, to colloquial in the second two.

The shift in the quality of the diction is clear enough. The first two lines are a generalized hortatory question phrased in terms that might do for an invocation to some minor deity of the wind; the second two lines are a specific and bitter exclamation phrased in the simplest language of common speech.

It is the metric pattern accompanying that shift of diction that is worth special attention:

> O Wes / tern wind, / / when wilt / thou blow
> That the small / rain down / may rain?
> Christ / , / that my love / were in / my arms
> And I / in my bed / again.

The first two lines make use of three spondees in seven feet, and of two series of three heavy stresses in a row. The second two lines make use of no spondees, there is no point in them where even two heavy stresses fall together, and there are two anapests in them as opposed to one in the first line, and there is a pyrrhic to add two more unstressed syllables between accents. The only unusual emphasis in the second two lines occurs in the monosyllabic foot at the beginning of line three (compare Frost's use of the same device after the fulcrum in "The Span of Life" and see the note on the passage). After that initial emphasis the meter becomes not only smooth but accelerated. It is as if that initial stress had consumed all the force of despair and passion, after which the voice can only slide forward into its grief.

Thus, one has located a first difference in the technical handling: the first two lines are metrically impeded and the second two lines are not only smooth but slightly accelerated. Having located that difference, one who wishes to experience poetry rather than simply to talk around it, will do well to consider that a fast passage in music is not the equivalent of a slow one, nor of the same passage repeated slowly. In the same way, a good poem does not change its pace without meaning something by that change. The rhythm is one part of the performance of the poem's "meaning."

The first two lines of the present poem, moreover, are impeded not only by the meter but by the four lingering "w" sounds followed by the open vowels of "thou blow" (which pick up the open vowel of the vocative at the beginning of the line), thus:

O WEHstern WInd HWEn WIlt thOU blOW.

With this much observed, one may identify the essence of the poem's performance of itself. It begins with a heavily impeded generalized invocation to the western wind of Spring. The poet draws out his cry as if tortured by the thought, carrying it on a rising inflection throughout the first two lines and leaving it suspended. The cry ends and the poet pauses, silent. Suddenly, within that silence, the terms of his grief change inside him. A second voice of his despair surges in him and lashes forth with a cry to Heaven. The voice resumes with a hammer-beat of anguish on the first syllable. Then, as if that first hammered syllable had drained the last strength of the speaker's anger, the voice slides off into a numb personal statement of the poet's exact grief, that grief now simply stated, no longer volatile and angry but defeated, and the metric line accordingly runs smooth and even accelerates in response to the fact that the poet no longer struggles against the truth, but closes on a dying fall.

Note that the foregoing paragraph is not a paraphrase of the poem, but rather a simplified description of the details of the poetic performance. The function of such description is not to replace the poem but to direct the attention to it by pointing out the emotional sequences of the poem in time and the accompanying shifts in technical management. The question to be addressed is always "How"—not "What"—does a poem mean?

In both "The Span of Life" and "O Western Wind" the poetic structure is built across a single fulcrum and the units on either side of the fulcrum are equal in length. The following poem ("The Fury of Aerial Bombardment," by Richard Eberhart) will illustrate a different case. Before one reads it, he needs to know that the poet served as an Instructor in Aerial Gunnery during World War II and that an essential part of such gunnery training consisted of memorizing the nomenclature of the many parts of a Browning .50 caliber machine gun. Obviously a gunner must be able to order repair parts from rear-area depots, and if he is to receive the right part he must be able to give its exact technical name, no matter how complicated. The "belt-feed-lever" and the "belt-holding-pawl" of the last line are two of the many items of nomenclature that student-gunners were required to study. Obviously the poet is bemused by the resemblance of such vocabulary exercises from the school-for-death to the exercises all children are assigned in the school-of-innocence.

> You would think the fury of aerial bombardment
> Would rouse God to relent; the infinite spaces
> Are still silent. He looks on shock-pried faces.
> History, even, does not know what is meant.
>
>   < 3
> You would feel that after so many centuries

God would give man to repent; yet he can kill
As Cain could, but with multitudinous will,
No farther advanced than in his ancient furies.

                                                      < 2

Was man made stupid to see his own stupidity?
Is God by definition indifferent, beyond us all?
Is the eternal truth man's fighting soul
Wherein the beast ravens in his own avidity?

                                                      < 1

Of Van Wettering I speak, and Averill,
Names on a list whose faces I do not recall.
But they are gone to early death, who late in school
Distinguished the belt-feed-lever from the belt-
      holding-pawl.

The principal fulcrum of this poem quite clearly occurs, as
marked, between the third and the fourth stanzas. There are
lesser fulcrums within the first three stanzas, but they are
better left for later discussion. The point to note is that there
is no reason for two statements to be of the same length in
order to have the same emotional weight. In many poems the
fulcrum occurs just before the last line, the single line thrust-
ing itself into balance with all that comes before.

The first three stanzas of "The Fury of Aerial Bombardment"
are made up of enormous rhetorical statements and questions
addressed to no less a subject than man's fate upon the planet.
In stanza four the address suddenly changes from a rhetoric for
abstract-man to an understated elegy for two boys named Van
Wettering and Averill, boys who sought no universal meaning
but simply distinguished the belt-feed-lever from the belt-
holding-pawl, and died of their schooling into the anonymities
of fate. They are not even faces; they are names on a list. The
only point at which they touch larger significance is that they
are gone to early death. Thus, they are unknowing heirs to
all human waste; their death is their one real illustration of

the universal questions the poem begins with. Yet the implication is clear that their death is both man's tragedy and
failure. The boys are the least of men in one sense, faceless
and forgotten; yet their deaths accuse all of mankind, the more
so in that these who die are so insignificant.[2]

There can be no mistaking that the author has changed
both his attitude toward the subject and his personal tone in
going from one side of the fulcrum to the other. The opening
attitude is one of the most intense moral indignation; the
opening tone is rhetorical and resonant enough for the loftiest
pulpit. The closing attitude drops the high moral indignation
in favor of the simplest sort of sorrow, and the tone changes
from high rhetoric to a conversational understatement. Inevitably the whole quality of the language changes from the
Latinate diction of moral abstraction, to the colloquial and less
Latinate diction of simple statement.

The change in the pace and the rhythm is as marked as the
change in diction. Each of the first three stanzas divides between masculine and feminine rhymes, the effect of the
feminine rhymes being to leave the voice suspended on a
rising inflection. The fourth stanza uses no such feminine
rhymes, each line closing on a firm masculine word. The voice
is brought down firm to the falling inflection.

The change in the quality of the metrics from one side of
the fulcrum to the other is even more emphatically marked.
Eberhart's meter is unusual for the number of light syllables
allowed into a single foot. One should sense at once that the
poem is written in pentameters. And despite great variation,
that the norm is iambic. (The next to the last line, though
lengthened to a hexameter, is made up entirely of iambics, and
may be taken as the rest-line of the poem, the line in which
the norm is most clearly asserted. When in doubt it is wise to
look for such rest-lines.) Against that norm, however, the voice
must swallow many accelerated syllables. So in the opening
line:

[2] *cf.* Spender's handling of the same theme in *Ultima Ratio Regum.*

Yoū woūld thínk / thē fu´ rȳ / of ae´ / rī āl /
bōm bárd mēnt

Line nine can be scanned only by allowing a double feminine foot at the end:

Wās mán / máde stū / pīd tō sée / hīs´ ówn / stū píd īt ȳ.

And line ten runs to seven light accents in the second and third feet:

Īs Gód / bȳ dē fíni tīon / īn dif fē rēnt, / / bēyónd /
ūs áll?

The characteristic of Eberhart's metric in the first three stanzas is extraordinary acceleration checked by relatively heavy caesura. The voice is thus required to lash out and stop, lash out and stop. The metric effect, when combined with the voice-thrust suggested by the vastness of the concepts being declared, is clearly oratorical. The rhythm thrusts like the voice of a man delivering a powerful, outraged sermon, and being carried away by it. Note, also, that the sermon concludes with the voice rising on a double feminine, appropriately in a question:

Whére in / thē Béast / ra´ vēns / īn hīs´ ówn /
ā´ vi dī tȳ?[3]

Across the fulcrum, on the other hand, there is only one case in which three light syllables fall together. The extraordinary accelerations have disappeared, the metric is much smoother, and the pace is further slowed by the fact that the last two lines have become hexameters. The extra foot of the hexameter in English seems almost invariably to slow the pace by drawing out the line.

[3] The first foot may with equal reason be taken as a pyrrhic. The syllables are equal whether taken as stressed or unstressed.

Ōf Vản / Wĕ ttēr īng / Ī spĕak, / ănd Á / vēr ĭll,
Nắmes / ōn ā̄ list, / / whōse fắ cēs / Ī dō nŏt /
   rē cȧll.
Būt thĕy / āre gŏne / tō ear / lȳ dĕath, / / whō
   lắte / iñ schŏol
Dīs tĭn / guīshed tħe bĕlt / fĕed lĕ vēr / / frōm
   tħē / bĕlt hŏld / īng pȧwl.[4]

Were the discussion of the poem to stop here, it would still be apparent that such changes in pace are not only relevant to the "meaning" of the poem, but so inseparably involved in the meaning that there can be no communication of the poem's essential experience until the voice has responded to the changes. Many sensitive readers are able to make such a response without being able to analyze why they have so responded; such attunement is the happy result of extensive and sensitive reading. It is possible, that is to say, to receive a poem without this sort of analysis. It is not possible, however, to *discuss* the poetic structure meaningfully without recognizing the countermoving balance of that structure across the fulcrum, and the attendant change in the handling of the poetic elements. It is precisely because paraphrase is incapable of taking these elements and their counterweights into account that one must go the long way round to the discussion if he truly wishes to know what the poem is doing with itself.

There still remains to be considered the matter of the lesser fulcrums in the structure of Eberhart's poem, the fulcrums numbered 2 and 3 as distinct from the major fulcrum numbered 1. Thus far the discussion has all been of central fulcrum points, of the poem divided in two. The suggested image of the poetic structure has been that of a scale-arm balanced across a single fulcrum. That image needs now to

---

[4] The beginning of line two may be scanned more regularly as a trochee followed by an iamb. There can be no doubt however that the normal speech rhythm of English makes "on a list" an anapest.

be expanded into something more like a piece of mobile sculpture, a structure possessing, to be sure, a single main point of balance, but containing further lesser balances within the parts.

Those lesser balances can become so intricate that to pursue all of them would lead to more confusion than clarity. Certainly, however, one may readily note that the first three stanzas of the Eberhart poem, though they constitute a single side of the central balance, are themselves divided into two units, one of which is divided once again. Represented as a diagrammatic mobile sculpture, with the numbers on the weights corresponding to the stanza numbers and F labeling the main fulcrum, the poem might be imagined thus:

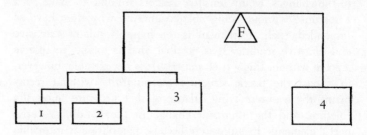

One has only to observe the carefully repeated pattern of stanzas one and two to recognize their close relationship. The first line of each stanza is a run-on and in each the voice continues without pause to a caesura after the third foot of the second line. After that caesura, the second lines of each stanza are again run-on, the voice in both cases coming to rest after the second foot of the third line. In both cases the voice once more moves forward for three feet and comes to rest again. And though the fourth line of the first stanza differs from the fourth line of the second by a small caesural effect around "even," the two lines are still more than sufficiently close to keep the pattern firm. Leaving that small caesural ripple around "even" out of consideration, one may diagram the pattern thus:

```
. . . . . . . . . . . . . . . . . .        m   f
. . . . . . . . . . . . . // . .           f   m
. . . . . . // . . . . . . . // .          f   m
. . . . . . . . . . . . . . // .           m   f
```

The rhyme, as indicated in the diagram by *m* for masculine and *f* for feminine, changes position from the first stanza (first column) to the second (second column) in a perfect reversed pattern.

And as if to leave no possible doubt that the stanzas are exactly related, the poet has added an unmissable and unusual internal rhyme—"relent-repent"—just before the first caesura in each stanza.

Such patterning of pauses and effects may again be recognized as characteristic of the rhetorician. The very parallel construction of the sentences—"You would think" in the first stanza, "You would feel" in the second, and again "Would rouse God" in the first, and "God would give" in the second are devices of the same rhetorical impulse.

Then, having established his pattern with such care, the poet breaks from it. The third stanza has a much more definite tendency to run the line straight to a full end-stop without internal pause, and thus the whole pattern of the pauses changes. A principal point of the present discussion, to repeat once again, is that such changes can only happen in response to a change in the poet's tone or attitude or both. He may realize exactly what change he is making, or he may simply follow the dictates of his feelings without analysis or need for analysis, but the changes themselves do not occur without cause. One can, of course, see at a glance that the voice has changed from making statements to asking questions. What one must also realize is that were he given no more than the scansion of the poem and its pattern of pauses, without a word of the text, he would still be able to tell that the voice had undergone some change in response to a change in the poet's tone and attitude.

If every poem is constructed on such countermotions across a fulcrum, and if the handling of the technical elements always changes from one unit of the poetic structure to another, the method of analysis here suggested must inevitably lead to a fuller understanding of that poetic structure. One need only locate the principal fulcrum, locate further the lesser fulcrums within the main units of the structure, and then analyze the differences in the handling of the poetic elements within each unit and sub-unit. To do that much, however, is not to have achieved the poem, but rather to have prepared oneself to achieve it. Any method of analysis is designed only to assure one that he is giving his human attention to the poem itself rather than to some nonpoetic paraphrase of its unenacted "meaning." In every good poem there is some final echo of nuance and feeling that lies beyond explanation and analysis.

Before this method can be aptly used, however, one must recognize that not all poems make their countermotions immediately apparent. It will be useful, therefore, to distinguish between *simple* and *complex* poems. Complex poems are of the order already discussed: they exist in countermotion across clearly perceivable fulcrums. Simple poems, on the other hand, travel in a straight line outward from the opening statement and seem to lack the counterthrust of an opposing idea or theme. The following ("My Papa's Waltz," by Theodore Roethke) is an example of a simple poem:

> The whiskey on your breath
> Could make a small boy dizzy;
> But I held on like death:
> Such waltzing is not easy.
>
> We romped until the pans
> Slid from the kitchen shelf;
> My mother's countenance
> Could not unfrown itself.

The hand that held my wrist
Was battered on one knuckle;
At every step I missed
My right ear scraped a buckle.

You beat time on my head
With a palm caked hard by dirt,
Then waltzed me off to bed
Still clinging to your shirt.

Despite its seeming lightness, "My Papa's Waltz" is a poem
of terror, all the more terrible because the boy is frightened
and hurt by the father even in play. "We romped," the poet
says, but the romp is a dizzying succession of painful glimpses:
the house is shaking, the mother is frowning, the father's hand
is scarred by violence, every misstep in the dance scrapes the
father's belt-buckle painfully across the boy's ear, and his head
is being pounded by that huge, hard palm. It is a romp, but
the boy must cling like death until he is finally dumped into
bed.

The terror, however, mounts in a straight line, detail upon detail, with no countermotion across a fulcrum *because there is no
change either in tone or in attitude.* The poem clearly breaks
into four parts, as indicated by the stanza breaks, but the parts
follow one another with no sense that one stanza break is more
important than another. And as one might suspect in such a
case, there is no marked difference in the handling of the
poetic elements from stanza to stanza. Metrics, pace, diction,
imagery, grammatical structure—all are very nearly constant
throughout. Even the pattern of pauses is the same from stanza
to stanza with only one variation in the extra pause at the
end of the third line of stanza one; with that exception all the
stanzas move without pause to the end of the second line,
and then move forward again without pause to the end of the
fourth line. And though there are two feminine rhymes in
the first and third stanzas, even they fall into a neatly repeated

pattern. The whole, disregarding the extra pause in stanza one, may be diagrammed thus:

```
. . . . . . . . . . . . . . . . .        m   m   m   m
. . . . . . . . . . . . . . //          f   m   f   m
. . . . . . . . . . . . . . . . .        m   m   m   m
. . . . . . . . . . . . . . //          f   m   f   m
```

The poem is simple, not because it lacks subtlety, but because it seems to lack a fulcrum. The fact is that the poem does indeed work against a fulcrum, but that *the fulcrum occurs after the last line*. Imagine, as a horrible example, that the poet had written an additional summarizing stanza in his first draft, and imagine that it had run to some such sad stuff as the following:

> Ah, that was long ago.
> Now, his first terrors shed,
> This dancer turns to go
> Calm, to the fearless dead.

Miserable and cliché-ridden poeticizing to be sure, but had such a stanza existed one would have had no hesitation in placing the fulcrum between it and the preceding poem, or in identifying the metric shift wherein three of the last four lines begin with monosyllabic feet.

The poet may very well have been tempted at first writing to add some such summarizing stanza. If so, he wisely put by the temptation in the secure sense that nothing could be said in such an addition that was not already better said by silence worked upon by the implications of the preceding lines. For silence, too, is a communication when placed in context. Thus *the fulcrum exists outside the poem, between the enacted experience and the silence that follows it*.

The following poem, on the other hand, is a fair example of a poem that over-ran its silence into six lines of "tacked-on moral," all the more painful in view of the extraordinary sharpness and economy of most of the poem up to those last six lines:

> Evening traffic homeward burns,
> Swift and even on the turns,
> Drifting weight in triple rows,
> Fixed relation and repose.
> This one edges out and by,
> Inch by inch with steady eye.
> But should error be increased,
> Mass and moment are released;
> Matter loosens, flooding blind,
> Levels driver to its kind.
>
> Ranks of nations thus descend,
> Watchful to a stormy end.
> By a moment's calm beguiled,
> I have got a wife and child.
> Fool and scoundrel guide the State.
> Peace is whore to Greed and Hate.
> Nowhere may I turn to flee:
> Action is security.
> Treading change with savage heel,
> We must live or die by steel.

A metric note is necessary before the discussion of the countermotions of this poem. The pattern of scansion for all lines is the same and may be represented thus:

$$| - | - | - |$$

Each line, that is, begins and ends with a heavy stress and each consists of four such heavy stresses enclosing three unstressed syllables. In such a case one may be uncertain whether to take the line as iambic or trochaic. The fact is that many English poets who have written in tetrameters have welcomed this effect as pleasing. The voice begins and ends each line on a stressed syllable and proceeds through each line without internal pause, the metronomic quality of such metrics producing an especially incantatory effect. It is relevant that this stress-to-stress pattern of the tetrameter line rarely, if ever, occurs when caesuras are used.

Despite any first uncertainty, however, the line is iambic, but with a truncated first foot. One has only to add a light syllable at the beginning of each line to see that iambic pattern:

> Aṡ évẹ / niṅg trá / ffic̄ hóme / wāꞯrd búrns
> Sō swíft / aꞯnd é / vēn ón / thē túrns

Obviously, however, such light syllables are not only metric excess baggage, but they interfere with the particular emphasis of the stress-to-stress pattern, loosening the incantatory effect. With something like the tolerance of the English ear to feminines before any full pause, the ear welcomes the dropping of these initial light syllables. Most precisely scanned, therefore, this tetrameter line might be represented as follows, with the comma indicating the truncated light syllable:

$$, \mid / - \mid / - \mid / - \mid$$

In such a special case of metronomic meter, it is unlikely that one will find any significant metric variation across the fulcrums of the poem. The only marked technical differences one may find between the poem and the last six lines are in the quality of the diction. With the last six lines omitted, however, the poem comes to a triumphant major balance (fulcrum) against its own following silence, and may be divided thus:

> Evening traffic homeward burns,
> Swift and even on the turns,

> Drifting weight in triple rows,
> Fixed relation and repose.
> This one edges out and by,
> Inch by inch with steady eye.
> But should error be increased,
> Mass and moment are released;
> Matter loosens, flooding blind,
> Levels driver to its kind.
>
>   < 2
>
> Ranks of nations thus descend,
> Watchful to a sudden end.
>
>   < 2
>
> By a moment's calm beguiled,
> I have got a wife and child.
>
>   < 1

The large fulcrum after the last couplet is labeled 1 to indicate that it is the major point of balance. The lesser fulcrums are both labeled 2 to indicate that they are equal to one another.

The first unit of the poem (up to the first fulcrum) is a dispassionate description of evening traffic seen primarily as a problem in physics: the tone of the passage is set by the implicit image of physical particles (detached from all human feeling) in motion. Rank on rank the particles move forward in their dangerous precision.

Across the first of the lesser fulcrums, the poet suddenly strikes a balance against his first image, amplifying the idea from literal description of traffic to an image-related idea of the condition of nations. "Nations" must certainly receive an unusually heavy stress by the logic of the implicit parallel construction. "Ranks of particles move toward collision and ranks of *nations* do exactly the same thing." The first shift then is from description to comment.

Having made a first comment on the largest scale, the poet pauses, and suddenly strikes a further balance with his material by applying it wryly to himself in the most personal terms. "By the moment's calm (fixed relation and repose) and like *nations*," the poet says, "*I* have also been beguiled." The three operative emphases are *physical particles, nations,* and *I.*

A triumphant poem thus far, a poetic structure lodging itself in a powerfully suggestive way against its following silence.

But at the end the moralist triumphs over the poet and the poem is blurred by six empty lines of abstract moralizing. "Fool, scoundrel, State, Peace, Greed, Hate" (and capitalized for emphasis) are terms that might have tempted such a pompous moralizer as Henley. There can certainly be no doubt that they constitute a change in the quality of the diction, but they are unfortunately a change for the worse.

For a poem must finally be seen as a formal structure in which the countermotions of the units *release into the silences they create a force of contained emotional perception beyond the power of statement.* The key terms are *release into silence, contained emotional perception,* and *statement.* The poetic structure *releases* its "meaning"; it does not *say* it.

THE SWAYING FORM: A PROBLEM
IN POETRY

by Howard Nemerov

I

The present essay is not an attempt to solve a problem so
much as an attempt to make certain that a problem of some
sort exists, and, if it does, to put it clearly before you. No
matter how many problems really exist—and now, as at all
times, there must be plenty of them—the world is always full
of people inventing problems simply as make-works for their
prefabricated solutions. As a friend of mine wrote in a prize-
winning poem at college, "We know the answers, but shall
we be asked the questions?" He has since become a novelist.

The problem I want to try to elucidate is most often discussed as one of belief, or of value, which is prior to poetry, and
the great instance of Dante's *Comedy* stands at the gate of the
discussion. It is usually argued on this basis that an explicit and
systematized belief is (a) intrinsically of value to the poet in
his composition and (b) a means for improving his communication with the mass of mankind.

Now I shall be taking up this theme by what many people
will consider to be the wrong end, and talking from the point
of view of the poet. My reflections are very far from being
impartial and objective, and positively invite objections, or even
cries of protest. I shall be suggesting, roughly, that the poet,
if he has not attained to a belief in the existence of God, has
at any rate got so far as to believe in the existence of the
world; and that this, sadly but truly, puts him, in the art of
believing, well out in front of many of his fellow-citizens,
who sometimes look as if they believed the existence of the
world to be pretty well encompassed in the sensations they

experience when they read a copy of *Time*. (These, by the way, are the people who, adapting a metaphor of Aristotle's, think of poetry as a gentle laxative for the emotions.)

So when I hear discussions, or see symptoms, of some *rapprochement* between religion and the arts—A has written a passion play in modern dress, B has composed an atonal oratorio, C has done murals for the little church in the home-town which he left thirty years ago to become a not quite first-rate cubist with a world reputation—my response is not one of unmixed happiness, and I incline to see, in the characteristic imagery of this period, religion and the arts as two great corporations, each composed of many subsidiary companies but both in roughly the same line of business, circling each other warily in the contemplation of a merger, wondering mean-while where the ultimate advantage will lie, and utterly unable to find out. To unfold a little this metaphor, I should say that in my view the persons seated around the conference table on this occasion are not the inventors of the product—not the prophets, saints, teachers, and great masters of art—but the usual vice-presidents, accountants, and lawyers on either side; the bishops and grand inquisitors, the critics and epimethean pedagogues who arbitrate these matters.

In other words, between ourselves and any clear view of the problematic area lies the Plain of Shinar, where the usual con-struction work is going forward vigorously, and the serious planners exchange their watchwords: "culture," "responsibil-ity," "values," and "communication." In this Babel, the word "religion" may mean "weekly attendance at the church of your choice," or it may mean the sort of thing that happened to Job—impossible to say. Similarly, the word "art" may be applied equally to the forty-eight preludes and fugues and to advertisements for whisky. That these things are so says noth-ing against either whisky or church attendance, but may be seriously damaging to art and religion.

Somewhere toward the beginning of things the two have a connection; as our somewhat frequently employed word "creative" will suggest. "Non merita il nome di creatore," said Tasso, "si non Iddio od il poeta." Clear enough: God and the poet alone deserve to be called creative, because they both create things. The recent history of this word is revealing: one reads, e.g., of "creative advertising," "creative packaging," and the possibility of becoming "a creative consumer." A dialect usage may be equally revealing: the mother says of her infant, "he is creating again," meaning either that the child is kicking up an awful fuss, or that he has soiled his diaper.

The relation of religion to more worldly activities is frequently characterized by extreme positions. To show what I hope I am not talking about, I shall give an example of each. Here is the extreme whereby religion, in seeking a connection with the world, becomes worldly itself:

SEES BOOM IN RELIGION, TOO
Atlantic City, June 23 (1957) AP.—President Eisenhower's pastor said tonight that Americans are living in a period of "unprecedented religious activity" caused partially by paid vacations, the eight-hour day, and modern conveniences.
"These fruits of material progress," said the Rev. Edward L. R. Elson of the National Presbyterian Church, Washington, "have provided the leisure, the energy, and the means for a level of human and spiritual values never before reached."

Despite an air of farcical silliness which will accompany any display of *hubris* which is at the same time unheroic, this statement—a kind of cartoonist's exaggeration of what one suspects is the real belief of many right-thinking persons—does fix the attention on a real question: whether it is possible for a religious attitude to exist in the acceptance of prosperity, and with its face set against suffering; a question near the heart of Christianity, and a question asked over and over, always to be answered negatively, in the Old Testament, where any statement that "the land had rest for so and so many years" is certain to be followed by the refrain, "And the children of Israel did evil *again* in the sight of the Lord, and served Baalim and Ashtaroth . . ."

The opposed extreme, wherein religion purifies itself quite out of the world, may likewise be identified by anecdote. At a conference on Elizabethan and seventeenth-century poetry, where a number of college students presented papers for discussion, the first three or four essays dealt with the lyrics of such poets as Campion and Herrick; after which a most serious young man arose, frowning, to say that his topic was George Herbert. He completed his impromptu introduction by saying, "We have heard a good deal this morning on the subject of *Love;* well, now we must turn our attention to an entirely different and more serious topic: *Religion.*" This inadvertence, I am sorry to say, seemed to me the revelation of something sad and true in attitudes bearing the official institutional name of religious attitudes. We might compare a remark of Yeats, that only two subjects are of interest to a serious intelligence: sex and the dead.

II

But our problem may be as easily obscured from the other side, the side which professes to be that of art, as from the side of religion. If we look to that great arena of the war of words where there are no poems but only Poetry, no paintings but only Art, we find statements of similar monolithic simplicity, which affect to find nothing problematic in the matter at all.

In that arena, for example, a well-known literary journalist has recently written (*New York Times* Book Review, May 3, 1959): "What the arts, literature included, need more than anything else just now, is a declaration of faith—faith in man's potentialities, faith in God, however you may conceive Him."

As a citizen, I may incline to accept the vague benevolence of all this. But as a practitioner of the art of writing, I am bored and disturbed by this sort of loose talk; just as I should probably be, were I a member of some religious community, by the pseudo-liberality of that casual rider to the idea of

God—"however you may conceive Him." Again we might compare the view of an artist, in the saying of Joseph Conrad that it is the object of art to render the highest kind of justice to the *visible world*: "It is above all, in the first place, to make you see."

By such exclusions I come to some definition of my theme: the elucidation of what things may be called religious in poetical works and in the professional attitude of the artist to the making of such works.

Even in this somewhat narrower definition, the problem is not easy to focus. I shall be trying to say that the artist's relation to spiritual and eternal things is comprised rather in the form of his work than in its message or its content; but that form is itself somewhat elusive, as I have indicated in titling these reflections "The Swaying Form" after the following passage in Florio's translation of Montaigne: "There is no man (if he listen to himselfe) that doth not discover in himselfe a peculiar forme of his, a swaying forme, which wrestleth against the art[1] and the institution, and against the tempest of passions, which are contrary unto him."

Florio's somewhat dreamlike English duplicates nicely the possibilities of Montaigne's phrase, "une forme maistresse." The form, that is, is simultaneously ruling and very variable, or fickle; shifting and protean as the form of water in a stream, where it is difficult or impossible to divide what remains from what runs away. The passage, read in this way, speaks of something in us which is double in nature, on both sides of things at once or by turns. And I would identify this "forme" with the impulse to art, the energy or libido which makes works of art. It is no paradox to say that the artistic impulse fights against "the art," for anyone who persists in this business knows that a part of his struggle is precisely against "the art," that is, against the accepted and settled standards of art in his time.

[1] The phrase about "the art" is not included in all editions.

So this "forme" has the following characteristics. It is (1)
allied with religion, for it is against "the tempest of passions"
and thus in favor of control, discipline, *askesis,* renunciation.
But it is (2) opposed to religion, for it is also against "the
institution," that is, against church, state, dogma, or any fixed
habit of the mind. Finally, it is (3) against something in its
own nature, called "the art," against, perhaps, the idea of
form itself.

For a curious tension exists between poetry and belief, idea,
principle, or reason. That is, while we hear a good deal about
poetry's need to be based upon an explicit view of the meaning
of existence, we are very often bored and exasperated by the
poetry which testifies to such a view, and incline to say that it
is bad poetry precisely in the degree that the poet has insisted
on referring the natural world to prior religious or philosophic
valuations.

Perhaps it will be illuminating now if I try to sum up
the swaying form, this complicated condition of the mind, by
imagining a poet at his table in the morning. He faces the
blank page, the page faces his mind—which, if it is not also a
blank, is a palimpsest on which fractions of world, which he
receives chiefly through language, are continually being recorded and erased and coming into strange, dissolving relations
to one another; these are, for the most part, not the consequential relations of thought, but rather insanely atomic instead.

To be piously in keeping with the values of the age, I
imagine this poet as asking himself, "What can I afford this
morning?" And going on to consider the possibilities, or impos-
sibilities: A little *saeva indignatio?* Something smart and severe
in a toga? A romantic pathos, or pathology, with wild glances
de chez Hölderlin? The dewy freshness of an early lyricism, say
about the period of Skelton and really, after all, noncommittal?
And so on, since the alternatives are very numerous.

There is only one, however, which now arises to give him
trouble: "How about me? Shall I be me? And who is that?"
He looks doubtfully at his tweeds, his grey flannels, stares at his

alert (but modern, but rootless) face in the mirror, and tries to
view that crew-cut in quick succession as a Franciscan tonsure,
an Augustan wig, a Romantic disorder. No good. He would
like to be himself, but acknowledges that himself is poetically
not what most interests him, nor what is likely to interest
others very much. Sighing, he wonders if poetry, if all great
effort in the world, does not involve a necessary hypocrisy (even
if one calls it, more politely, not hypocrisy but drama or metaphor, a necessary approach by analogy), and now he gratefully
recalls having read somewhere (it was in Castiglione, but he
likes the elegant indolence of "somewhere") that Julius Caesar
wore a laurel crown to disguise the fact that he was bald. Encouraged a little, he jots down a note reducing to iambic pentameter mighty Caesar—

Who hid his baldness in a laurel crown

—and adds, in prose, "Poets do this, too." Comforted, he occu-
pies the rest of the morning contemplating the publication of a
small volume of epigrams on this theme. But come lunchtime,
his wife having uncanned a can of alphabet soup which seems
to him the image of his condition, the problem remains: Hypocrisy. Seeming, Angelo, seeming. The truest poetry is the most
feigning. But is it, really? And how shall we edify the common
reader this afternoon? By being Plato? Moody and Sankey? The
Pope? Alexander Pope? How shall we solve the problems of
society? Affirm the eternal verities? Become rich and famous
and sought-after for our opinions (the filing cabinet is full of
them) on all sorts of important themes?

No, this will never do. Hypocrisy merges with cynicism.
Where is that portrait of Keats?

And so the weary circle begins again. Only once in a
while it opens, as something comes into his head and he suddenly commits a poem. At that time, curiously, he does not
worry in the least about whether this poem faithfully represents himself, his beliefs, values, tensions, or the absence of all
these. He simply writes the poem.

By this ordinary anguish, occasionally relieved in action, a great deal of literature, both good and bad, gets itself produced.

The troubles of this hypothetical or generalized poet will perhaps strike some of you as very literary, over-educated, or even positively neurasthenic, and you may be inclined to say impatiently to him, "Fool, look in thy heart and write," not caring to consider that when Sir Philip Sidney made this excellent recommendation, he was speaking, just like our poet, to himself. And, too, such is the confusion over these things, instructions to look in one's heart and write may turn out translated for practical purposes in weird ways, e.g.: "Look in thy heart and be big, free and sloppy, like Whitman, who is now becoming fashionable again." There is no end, except for that poem once in a while, to the poet's ability at perverting sound doctrine.

If the foregoing description is even partly applicable to the poetic process, it will be plain that the world will wait a long time for "a declaration of faith" in the poems of this poet. It may also be a consequence of his problem with his identity that a good deal of modern poetry is poetry about the problem, poetry which reveals to interpretation one reflective dimension having to do with the process of composition itself. This development, where the mind curves back upon itself, may be always a limit, not only for poetry but for every kind of thought, for that "speculation" which Shakespeare says "turns not to itself till it hath travel'd and is mirror'd there where it may see itself," adding that "this is not strange at all." But perhaps it has become more strange in the present age, that palace of mirrors where, says Valéry, the lonely lamp is multiplied, or where, as Eliot says, we multiply variety in a wilderness of mirrors, and where the "breakthrough," so pathetically and often discussed in relation to all contemporary arts, is most faithfully imagined in Alice's adventure through the looking-glass, the last consequence of narcissism and "incest of spirit" (Allen Tate, "Last Days of Alice") being the explosion into absurdity, very frequently followed by silence.

Silence, alas, may be preferable to the demand of "educators" that the poet should affirm something (anything?) or the often iterated instruction of certain literary persons that he should *communicate* (what?). But silence, for anyone who has set out to be a poet, is an unlovely alternative, containing in itself some religious (that is, some sinful) implication of being too good for this world, so that many poets accept the disabilities of their elected condition by making many small refusals to prevent one great one. The vanities of publication, these seem to say, are better than the silences of pride. And so, for them, the weary round begins again after every poem, as they seek over and over an image of their being: hermit crabs, crawling unprotected from one deserted shell to the next, finding each time a temporary home which, though by no means a perfect fit, is better at any rate than their nakedness.

It is gratuitous, or even impertinent after all this, and surely offers no defense, to say that they sometimes write good poems in their planetary course from house to house. What can we possibly mean, now, by *a good poem?* Let that be another circle, in another hell. While the present purpose is to say something about the process itself, the kind of relation with the world which results in poetic writings and is an attempt to fix for a moment the swaying form.

III

When people are impatient with a work of art they assert their feeling in this way: "What does it mean?" Their tone of voice indicates that this is the most natural question in the world, the demand which they have the most immediate and God-given right to make. So their absolute condemnation and dismissal of a work of art is given in this way: "It doesn't mean anything. It doesn't mean anything *to me.*" Only in those plaintive last words does there appear a tiny and scarcely acknowledged doubt of the all-sufficiency of this idea of mean- ing—that there may actually be meanings, which one does not personally possess.

Now we are all forced to believe about large areas of the

world's work that this is so: that all around us physicists, financiers, and pharmacists are conducting complex operations which do have meaning though we do not know what it is. While we may occasionally wonder if those emperors are in fact wearing any clothes, we more usually allow that our bewilderment belongs to ourselves and does not say anything destructive about those disciplines in themselves, even where they do not produce any overwhelmingly obvious practical result such as an atomic explosion. But about works of art we continue to ask that question, "what do they mean?" and regard the answer to it as somehow crucial.

In a realm of contemplation, the question about meaning could, though it generally does not, begin a chain reaction involving the whole universe, since the answer can be given only in terms to which the same question is again applicable. But because we are well-mannered people, or because we haven't the time, or really don't care, or because we are in fact reassured and consoled by receiving an answer—any answer— we know where to stop. So that a large part of our intellectual operations takes inevitably the following form:

A. Why is the grass green?

B. Because of the chlorophyll.

A. Oh.

So, in a realm of contemplation, meaning would itself be inexplicable. The typewriters rattle, the telephones ring, the moving finger keeps writing one triviality after another, the great gabble of the world goes incessantly on as people translate, encipher, decipher, as one set of words is transformed more or less symmetrically into another set of words—whereupon someone says, "O, now I understand. . . ."

But the question about meaning attests, wherever it is asked, the presence of civilization with all its possibilities, all its limitations; attests the presence of *language,* that vast echoing rattle and sibilance, buzzing between ourselves and whatever it is we presume we are looking at, experiencing, being in, and which sometimes appears to have an independent value, if any at all, like the machine someone built a few years back, which had thousands of moving parts and no function. The semanticist to the contrary, words are things, though not always the things they say they are. The painter Delacroix expressed it by saying that Nature is a dictionary. Everything is there, but not in the order one needs. The universe itself, so far as we relate ourselves to it by the mind, may be not so much a meaning as a rhythm, a continuous articulation of question and answer, question and answer, a musical dialectic precipitating out moments of meaning which become distinct only as one wave does in a sea of waves. "You think you live under universal principles," said Montaigne, "but in fact they are municipal bylaws."

Language, then, is the marvelous mirror of the human condition, a mirror so miraculous that it can see what is invisible, that is, the relations between things. At the same time, the mirror is a limit, and as such it is sorrowful; one wants to break it and look beyond. But unless we have the singular talent for mystical experience we do not really break the mirror, and even the mystic's experience is available to us only as reflected, inadequately, in the mirror. Most often man deals with reality by its reflection. That is the sense of Perseus' victory over the Gorgon by consenting to see her only in the mirror of his shield, and it is the sense of the saying in Corinthians that we see now as through a glass darkly—a phrase rendered by modern translators as "now we see as in a little mirror."

Civilization, mirrored in language, is the garden where relations grow; outside the garden is the wild abyss. Poetry, an art of fictions, illusions, even lies—"Homer," said Aristotle, "first taught us the art of framing lies in the right way"—poetry is the art of contemplating this situation in the mirror of language.

"Only connect . . ." is the civilized and civilizing motto of a book by E. M. Forster, where he speaks eloquently of meaning, art and order in "the world of telegrams and anger," and of what exists outside that world: "panic and emptiness, panic and emptiness." W. H. Auden, also very eloquently, writes of the limiting extremes within which meaning means, between "the ocean flats where no subscription concerts are given" and "the desert plain where there is nothing for lunch."

But meaning, like religion, seeks of its own nature to monopolize experience. For example, in children's playbooks there are numbered dots to be followed in sequence by the pencil; the line so produced finally becomes recognizable as a shape. So the lines produced among stars (which can scarcely all be in the same plane) become the geometrical abstractions of a Bear, a Wagon, Orion the Hunter, and by softening or humanizing the outlines, recognizable images are produced, but in the process the stars themselves have to be omitted. So does meaning at first simplify and afterward supersede the world. Poetry, I would say, is, in its highest ranges, no mere playing with the counters of meaning, but a perpetual rederiving of the possibility of meaning from matter, of the intelligible world from the brute recalcitrance of things. Poetry differs from thought in this respect, that thought eats up the language in which it thinks. Thought is proud, and always wants to forget its humble origin in things. In doing so, it begins to speak by means of very elevated abstractions which quickly become emptied and impoverished. The business of poetry is to bring thought back into relation with the five wits, the five senses which Blake calls "the chief inlets of soul in this age," to show how our discontents, as Shakespeare finely says of Timon's, "are unremovably coupled to nature." So the ivory tower must always be cut from the horn of Behemoth.

The relation of poetry to religion is both intimate and antithetical, for poetry exists only by a continuing revelation in a world always incarnate of word and flesh indissolubly, a world simultaneously solid and transpicuous. At the same time, religion can never really dissociate itself from poetry and the continuing revelation, and its attempts to do so turn it into a form of literary criticism, as the scriptures and sacred books of the world, in comparison with their interminable commentaries, will sufficiently show. Poetry and institutionalized religion are in a sense the flowing and the static forms of the same substance, liquid and solid states of the same elemental energy.

This is a simple thing; it has been said many times and forgotten many times plus one. William Blake says it this way:

> The ancient Poets animated all sensible objects with Gods or Geniuses, calling them by the names and adorning them with the properties of woods, rivers, mountains, lakes, cities, nations, and whatever their enlarged and numerous senses could perceive.
>
> And particularly they studied the Genius of each city and country, placing it under its Mental Deity;
>
> Till a system was formed, which some took advantage of, and enslav'd the vulgar by attempting to realise or abstract the Mental Deities from their objects—thus began Priesthood;
>
> Choosing forms of worship from poetic tales.
>
> And at length they pronounc'd that the Gods had order'd such things.
>
> Thus men forgot that All Deities reside in the Human Breast.

The poet's business, I would say, is to name as accurately as possible a situation, but a situation which he himself is in. The name he gives ought to be so close a fit with the actuality it summons into being that there remains no room between inside and outside; the thought must be "like a beast moving in its skin" (Dante). If he does his work properly, there won't be any other name for the situation (and for his being in it) than the one he invents, or, rather, his name will swallow up all the others as Aaron's rod swallowed up the rods of Pharaoh's wizards.

Sometimes the name so given is a relatively simple one, as when Alexander Pope gave the Prince of Wales a dog, and had inscribed on its collar:

> I am his Highness' dog at Kew.
> Pray tell me, sir, whose dog are you?

And sometimes the name so given, the situation thus identified and brought into being, is immensely complex, so that one has to refer to it by a tag, an abbreviation, e.g., "King Lear."

A poem, whether of two lines or ten thousand, is therefore the name of something, and in its ideal realm of fiction or illusion it corresponds to what is said of the Divine Name in several significant respects:

> *It is unique.*
> *It can never be repeated.*
> *It brings into being the situation it names, and is therefore truly a creation.*
> *It is secret, even while being perfectly open and public, for it defines a thing which could not have been known without it.*

As to the poet himself, one might add this. Writing is a species of *askesis,* a persevering devotion to the energy passing between self and world. It is a way of living, a way of being, and, though it does produce results in the form of "works," these may come to seem of secondary importance to the person so engaged.

The young writer is always told (he was, anyhow, when I was young) that writing means first and last "having something to say." I cherish as a souvenir of boyhood that honorable and aged platitude, but would like to modify it by this addition: writing means trying to find out what the nature of things has to say about what you think you have to say. And the process is reflective or cyclical, a matter of feedback between oneself and "it," an "it" which can gain its identity only in the course of being brought into being, come into being only in the course of finding its identity. This is a matter, as Lu Chi says, of how to hold the axe while you are cutting its handle.

I say that writing is a species of *askesis.* But as it works in an ideal or fictional, rather than in a practical, realm, so it purifies not the character but the style. There is, however, a connection between the two, at least in the hope that a charity of the imagination shall be not quite the same thing as an imaginary charity.

IV

That, then, is what I have tried to characterize as "the swaying form," a process of becoming related to nature and the nature of things (*natura naturata* and *natura naturans*). The view here taken suggests that art has some evident affinities with both religion and science on the very simple basis that all three exist in the presumption that the truth is possible to be told about existence; but these affinities themselves also define differences, distances, and intrinsic antagonisms.

As to art's relation with science. The experimental method was defined, by Galileo, I believe, as putting nature to the question, where "the question" meant the judicial process of torture. The definition seems to imply a faith that nature, so treated, will reveal the secret name for a situation; when once that situation has been isolated, treated as a situation in itself and considered for a moment apart from the flux of all things, nature will, as it were, confess her presumably guilty secret.

Well, the artist, it seems to me, works on a not so different principle, leading from hypothesis—"what will happen to this noble nature if it can be led to believe Desdemona unfaithful?" —through experiment—the question as put by Iago—to result, to "the tragic loading of this bed." In this sense, and not in the fashionable popular sense, art is "experimental," and its methods to a certain extent resemble those of the laboratory; art, too, produces its process under controlled and limiting conditions, cutting away irrelevancies, speeding up or slowing down the reaction under study, so that the results, whatever they may be, will stand forth with a singular purity and distinction. The instruments of science, of course, have as their aim the creation of an objectivity as nearly as possible universal in character; the poet's aim might be thought of as the same and reversed, a mirror image—to represent in the world the movement of a subjectivity as nearly as possible universal in character.

And art is akin to religion, if we will be non-denominational about it, in that the work (though not, perhaps, the artist, oddly enough) is driven by its own composition to the implication of invisible things inherent in visible ones. The subject, the content, of the art work is sorrowful, because life is sorrowful; but the work itself, by the nature of its form, dances. A beautiful passage from Proust's novel will be relevant here. Marcel is thinking of the writer Bergotte, who died of a stroke while contemplating a detail, a piece of yellow wall, in a painting by Vermeer:

> He was dead. Forever? Who can say? After all, occult experiences demonstrate no more than the dogmas of religion do about the soul's continuance. But what can be said is this, that we live our life as though we had entered it under the burden of obligations already assumed in another; there is, in the conditions of our life here, no reason which should make us believe ourselves obliged to do good, to be fastidious or even polite, nor which should make the godless painter believe himself obliged to start over twenty times a detail the praise of which will matter very little to his body eaten by worms—a detail such as the section of yellow wall painted with such skill and taste by an artist forever unknown and scarce identified under the name of Vermeer. All such obligations, which have no sanction in our present life, seem to belong to a different world based on goodness, consideration and sacrifice, a world altogether different from this one, and from which we emerge to be born on this earth, before perhaps returning there to live under the rule of those unknown laws which we have obeyed because we carry their teaching within us though unaware who traced it there—those laws to which every profound work of the intelligence tends to reconcile us, and which are invisible only—and forever!—to fools.

So the work of art is religious in nature, not because it beautifies an ugly world or pretends that a naughty world is a nice one—for these things especially art does not do—but because it shows of its own nature that things drawn within the sacred circle of its forms are transfigured, illuminated by an inward radiance which amounts to goodness because it amounts to being itself. In the life conferred by art, Iago and Desdemona, Edmund and Cordelia, the damned and the blessed, equally achieve immortality by their relation with the creating intelligence which sustains them. The art work is not responsible for saying that things in reality are so, but rather for revealing what this world says to candid vision. It is thus that we delight in tragedies whose actions in life would merely appall us. And it is thus that art, by its illusions, achieves a human analogy to the resolution of that famous question of theodicy—the relation of an Omnipotent Benevolence to evil—which the theologians, bound to the fixed forms of things, have for centuries struggled with, intemperately and in vain. And it is thus that art, by vision and not by dogma, patiently and repeatedly offers the substance of things hoped for, the evidence of things unseeen.

THE POETRY OF LOUISE BOGAN

by Theodore Roethke

Two of the charges most frequently leveled against poetry by women are lack of range—in subject matter, in emotional tone —and lack of a sense of humor. And one could, in individual instances among writers of real talent, add other esthetic and moral shortcomings: the spinning-out; the embroidering of trivial themes; a concern with the mere surfaces of life—that special province of the feminine talent in prose—hiding from the real agonies of the spirit; refusing to face up to what existence is; lyric or religious posturing; running between the boudoir and the altar, stamping a tiny foot against God; or lapsing into a sententiousness that implies the author has reinvented integrity; carrying on excessively about Fate, about time; lamenting the lot of the woman; caterwauling; writing the same poem about fifty times, and so on.

But Louise Bogan is something else. True, a very few of her earliest poems bear the mark of fashion, but for the most part she writes out of the severest lyrical tradition in English. Her real spiritual ancestors are Campion, Jonson, the anonymous Elizabethan song writers. The word order is usually direct, the plunge straight into the subject, the music rich and subtle (she has one of the best ears of our time), and the subject in- variably given its due and no more. As a result, her poems, even the less consequential, have a finality, a comprehensive- ness, the sense of being all of a piece, that we demand from the short poem at its best.

The body of her complete poetic work is not great, but the "range," both emotional and geographical, is much wider than might be expected from a lyric poet. There is the brilliant (and exact) imagery of her New England childhood; there is also the highly formal world of Swift's Ireland; the rich and baroque background of Italy called up in the evocative "Italian Morning." And, of course, her beloved Austria. Her best lyrics, unlike so much American work, have the sense of a civilization behind them—and this without the deliberate piling up of exotic details, or the taking over of a special, say Grecian, vocabulary.

Invariably these effects are produced with great economy, with the exact sense of diction that is one of the special marks of her style. Even out of context, their power, I believe, is evident. Thus, in "Hypocrite Swift," a curious *tour de force* which incorporates many actual phrases from Swift's *Journal to Stella,* there suddenly occurs the stanza:

> On walls at court, long gilded mirrors gaze.
> The parquet shines; outside the snow falls deep.
> Venus, the Muses stare above the maze.
> Now sleep.

For one terrifying instant we are within Swift's mind, in eighteenth-century Ireland, sharing the glitter, the horror and glory of his madness.

Again, from the poem, "Italian Morning," the lines:

> The big magnolia, like a hand,
> Repeats our flesh. (O bred to love,
> Gathered to silence!) In a land
> Thus garnished, there is time enough
>
> To pace the rooms where painted swags
> Of fruit and flower in pride depend,
> Stayed as we are not.

The "garnished" and the "painted swags" are triumphs of exactitude in language—suggest the elaborate background without recourse to merely baroque diction.

This is only one, and by no means the best, of Miss Bogan's poems on time, on change, on the cessation of time. Even in her earliest work, she seems to be seeking a moment when things are caught, fixed, frozen, seen, for an instant, under the eye of eternity.

A very early piece, "Decoration," printed in her first book, *Body of This Death,* but not in the *Collected,* is, I believe, a beginning, a groping toward this central theme:

> A macaw preens upon a branch outspread
> With jewelry of seed. He's deaf and mute.
> The sky behind him splits like gorgeous fruit
> And claw-like leaves clutch light till it has bled.
> The raw diagonal bounty of his wings
> Scrapes on the eye color too chafed. He beats
> A flattered tail out against gauzy heats;
> He has the frustrate look of cheated kings.
> And all the simple evening passes by:
> A gillyflower spans its little height
> And lovers with their mouths press out their grief.
> The bird fans wide his striped regality
> Prismatic, while against a sky breath-white
> A crystal tree lets fall a crystal leaf.

This is a vulnerable poem, in spite of certain felicities (the fine "and all the simple evening passes by," for instance). But the uncharitable might say hardly beyond magazine verse. And even though Miss Bogan disarms us with her title, the poem remains *too* static, not very interesting syntactically, and the final line plays upon one of the clichés of the twenties: "A crystal tree lets fall a crystal leaf." Still, the scene is looked at steadily and closely; the poem is what it is.

Another early piece, "Statue and the Birds," is already a much better poem on essentially the same theme. However, the "Medusa," printed on the page opposite "Decoration" in the first book, is a breakthrough to great poetry, the whole piece welling up from the unconscious, dictated as it were:

I had come to the house, in a cave of trees,
Facing a sheer sky.
Everything moved,—a bell hung ready to strike,
Sun and reflection wheeled by.

When the bare eyes were before me
And the hissing hair,
Held up at a window, seen through a door.
The stiff bald eyes, the serpents on the forehead
Formed in the air.

This is a dead scene forever now.
Nothing will ever stir.
The end will never brighten it more than this,
Nor the rain blur.

The water will always fall, and will not fall,
And the tipped bell make no sound.
The grass will always be growing for hay
Deep on the ground.

And I shall stand here like a shadow
Under the great balanced day,
My eyes on the yellow dust, that was lifting in
   the wind,
And does not drift away.

Now, what does this poem mean?—in final terms? It could
be regarded, simply, as a poem of hallucination—a rare enough
thing—that maintains its hold on the reader from the very
opening lines to the end. But we are told some other things,
with the repetitiousness of obsession: "I had come to the
house, in a *cave* of trees": the house itself is in a cave, a
womb within a womb, as it were. But notice: "facing a sheer
sky"—obviously the "scene" is being played against a backdrop
of heaven, of eternity, with everything moving yet not moving—"the bell hung ready to strike."

Then the terrifying moment: "the bare eyes," "the hissing hair," of the *anima,* the Medusa, the man-in-the-woman, mother—*her* mother, possibly—again "held up at a *window,"* "*seen* through a *door":* certainly feminine symbols. And notice, "the stiff bald eyes, the serpents on the forehead formed in the air"—in *erectus,* in other words.

The last three stanzas bring us the self-revelation, the terrible finality of the ultimately traumatic experience. I shan't labor the interpretation further, except—why "yellow dust"? To me, it suggests the sulphurous fires of hell, here under the sheer sky of eternity.

I suggest that this is a great lyric and in an area of experience where most writers are afraid to go—or are incapable of going.

Miss Bogan is a contender, an opponent, an adversary, whether it be the devouring or overpowering mother, or time itself. And she can quarrel with her *daemon,* her other self, as in "Come, Break With Time." Here she manages with great skill the hortatory tone, the command—from which so much bogus poetry often results.

> Come, break with time,
> You who were lorded
> By a clock's chime
> So ill afforded.
> If time is allayed
> Be not afraid.
>
> *I shall break, if I will.*
> Break, since you must.
> Time has its fill,
> Sated with dust.
> Long the clock's hand
> Burned like a brand.

> Take the rocks' speed
> And Earth's heavy measure.
> Let buried seed
> Drain out time's pleasure,
> Take time's decrees.
> Come, cruel ease.

Notice the remarkable shift in rhythm in the last stanza, with the run-on lines that pick up the momentum of the poem. We are caught up in the earth's whole movement; I am reminded, perhaps eccentrically, of Wordsworth's

> No motion has she now, no force;
>   She neither hears nor sees;
> Rolled round in earth's diurnal course
>   With rocks, and stones, and trees.

In this instance, I feel one poem supports, gives additional credence, to the other.

Yet Miss Bogan does not rest with that effect. There is a terrible irony in "Let buried seed/drain out time's pleasure." Then the acceptance that all humans must make: "Take time's decrees." The last line remains for me a powerful ambiguity. Is she like Cleopatra, or Keats, asking for easeful death, or the cruel ease of unawareness, of insentience, of the relief from time that old age provides? There is, of course, no final answer, and none is necessary.

One definition of a serious lyric—it may come from Stanley Kunitz—would call it a revelation of a tragic personality. Behind the Bogan poems is a woman intense, proud, strong-willed, never hysterical or silly; who scorns the open unabashed caterwaul so usual with the love poet, male or female; who never writes a serious poem until there is a genuine "upwelling" from the unconscious; who shapes emotion into an inevitable-seeming, an endurable, form.

For love, passion, its complexities, its tensions, its betrayals,
is one of Louise Bogan's chief themes. And this love, along with
marriage itself, is a virtual battleground. But the enemy is
respected, the other is *there,* given his due; the experience,
whatever its difficulties, shared.

Thus, in "Old Countryside":

Beyond the hour we counted rain that fell
On the slant shutter, all has come to proof.
The summer thunder, like a wooden bell,
Rang in the storm above the mansard roof,

And mirrors cast the cloudy day along
The attic floor; wind made the clapboards creak.
You braced against the wall to make it strong,
A shell against your cheek.

Long since, we pulled brown oak-leaves to the ground
In a winter of dry trees; we heard the cock
Shout its unplaceable cry, the axe's sound
Delay a moment after the axe's stroke.

Far back, we saw, in the stillest of the year,
The scrawled vine shudder, and the rose-branch show
Red to the thorns, and, sharp as sight can bear,
The thin hound's body arched against the snow.

This, it need hardly be said, is typical Bogan: the concern
with time, the setting put down with great exactitude, the
event re-created and then looked back upon—the whole thing
vivid in the mind's eye, in the memory. The details are no mere
accretion, but are developed with a cumulative surprise and
the power of great art.

Notice the oracular, almost Shakespearean finality of "all has
come to proof"—and this, at the start of a poem. She announces
boldly but not portentously, and we believe. Notice, too, the
mastery of the epithet—the cock's "unplaceable cry," the

"scrawled vine," the rose-branch "red to the thorns." And then the final triumph of the last image, upon which everything hinges: "The thin hound's body arched against the snow."

But what has come to proof? We are not told, explicitly, nor should we be. Invariably, the final experience, however vivid and exact the imagery, comes to us obliquely. It stays with us, can be brooded upon, and brought, finally, into our own lives.

This obliquity, at once both Puritan and feminine, brings Louise Bogan close, despite differences in temperament, to Emily Dickinson and to Marianne Moore. None quails before the eye of eternity; their world is their own, sharply defined. If others enter it, the arrival, the meeting, is on their terms.

Many of the best Bogan poems in this vein are of such complexity and depth that the excerpt is virtually impossible, particularly since Miss Bogan often employs the single developed image with usually at least two levels of meaning. And often within a very short space, she effects an almost intolerable tension, a crescendo in rhythm, as in "Men Loved Wholly Beyond Wisdom"; or builds up the theme powerfully, as in the remarkable "Feuer-Nacht," and then takes a chance with a generalization without losing the momentum of the poem:

> To touch at the sedge
> And then run tame
> Is a broken pledge.
> The leaf-shaped flame
> Shears the bark piled for winter,
> The grass in the stall.
> Sworn to lick at a little,
> It has burned all.

Some of her best pieces begin with the object perceived, as it were, for an instant, and the image remembered, fixed in the mind unforgettably.

However, she is not, as I have said, a poet of the immediate moment, as say, Lawrence, but of the time *after,* when things come into their true focus, into the resolution, the final perspective. Listen to "Roman Fountain":

> Up from the bronze, I saw
> Water without a flaw
> Rush to its rest in air,
> Reach to its rest, and fall.
>
> Bronze of the blackest shade,
> An element man-made,
> Shaping upright the bare
> Clear gouts of water in air.
>
> O, as with arm and hammer,
> Still it is good to strive
> To beat out the image whole,
> To echo the shout and stammer
> When full-gushed waters, alive,
> Strike on the fountain's bowl
> After the air of summer.

For me, the opening lines are one of the great felicities of our time: the thing put down with an ultimate exactness, absolutely as it is. Perhaps the two appositives "Bronze of the blackest shade/ An element man-made" in the next stanza are a bit "written"; but "gouts of water" saves everything. Nor do I care much for the evocative outcry—and the arm and hammer image. Yet the poem resolves itself with characteristic candor. We have come a long way in a short space.

I believe this poem will stay in the language: its opening alone demands immortality. Yet it exists, too, as a superb piece of observation; as a phallic poem; as a poem about the nature of the creative act in the no-longer young artist.

In the last lines of this piece, we hear the accent of the later work: a tone of resignation, an acceptance of middle age, a comment, often, on the ironies of circumstance. Of these, I believe "Henceforth, From the Mind" to be a masterpiece, a poem that could be set beside the best work of the Elizabethans:

> Henceforth, from the mind,
> For your whole joy, must spring
> Such joy as you may find
> In any earthly thing,
> And every time and place
> Will take your thought for grace.
>
> Henceforth, from the tongue,
> From shallow speech alone,
> Comes joy you thought, when young,
> Would wring you to the bone,
> Would pierce you to the heart
> And spoil its stop and start.
>
> Henceforward, from the shell,
> Wherein you heard, and wondered
> At oceans like a bell
> So far from ocean sundered—
> A smothered sound that sleeps
> Long lost within lost deeps,
>
> Will chime you change and hours,
> The shadow of increase,
> Will sound you flowers
> Born under troubled peace—
> Henceforth, henceforth
> Will echo sea and earth.

And certainly, "Song," "Homunculus," and "Kept," at the very least, are among our best short lyrics. We are told:

> Time for the pretty clay,
> Time for the straw, the wood.
> The playthings of the young
> Get broken in the play,
> Get broken, as they should.

And, in terms of personal revelation, "The Dream" might be regarded as a later companion piece to "Medusa." In some of these last poems, as "After the Persian," "Song for the Last Act," the rhythms, the music, are richly modulated, highly stylized, grave and slow. Miss Bogan is not repeating herself, but moving into another world. There is no lessening of her powers.

I find my rather simple method of "pointing out"—at which Miss Marianne Moore is such a master—has omitted or under-emphasized certain qualities in Louise Bogan's work, and of necessity passed by remarkable poems.

For example, the great variety and surety of her rhythms—that clue to the energy of the psyche. Usually the movement of the poem is established in the very first lines, as it should be:

> If ever I render back your heart,
>   So long to me delight and plunder

or

> To me, one silly task is like another
> I bare the shambling tricks of lust and pride

And she is a master of texture, yet always the line is kept firm: she does not lapse into "sound" for the sake of sound, lest the poem thin out into loose "incantatory" effects. Thus:

> Under the thunder-dark, the cicadas resound

or the grave rhythm of

The measured blood beats out the year's delay

or in "Winter Swan":

It is a hollow garden, under the cloud;
Beneath the heel a hollow earth is turned;
Within the mind the live blood shouts aloud;
Under the breast the willing blood is burned,
Shut with the fire passed and the fire returned.

Louise Bogan rarely, if ever, repeats a cadence, and this in
an age when some poets achieve a considerable reputation
with two or three or even *one* rhythm. The reason for this is,
I believe, her absolute loyalty to the particular emotion, which
can range from the wry tenderness and humor of "A Crossed
Apple" to the vehemence of "Several Voices Out of a Cloud":

Come, drunks and drug-takers; come, perverts unnerved!
Receive the laurel, given though late, on merit; to whom
　　and wherever deserved.

Parochial punks, trimmers, nice people, joiners true-blue,
Get the hell out of the way of the laurel. It is deathless
　　And it isn't for you.

This, for me, incorporates the truly savage indignation of
Swift—and still manages to be really funny. And even in a
poem on a "high" theme, "I Saw Eternity," she can say:

　　　　Here, mice, rats,
　　　　Porcupines and toads,
　　　　Moles, shrews, squirrels,
　　　　Weasels, turtles, lizards,—
　　　　Here's bright Everlasting!
　　　　Here's a crumb of Forever!
　　　　Here's a crumb of Forever!

I have said that Miss Bogan has a sharp sense of objects, the eye that can pluck out from the welter of experience the inevitable image. And she loves the words, the nouns particularly, rich in human association. "Baroque Comment" ends:

> Crown and vesture; palm and laurel chosen as noble
>   and enduring;
> Speech proud in sound; death considered sacrifice;
> Mask, weapon, urn; the ordered strings;
> Fountains; foreheads under weather-bleached hair;
> The wreath, the oar, the tool,
> The prow;
> The turned eyes and the opened mouth of love.

But let us see how this side of her talent operates when she is absolutely open, as in the deeply moving elegy "To My Brother":

> O you so long dead,
> You masked and obscure,
> I can tell you, all things endure:
> The wine and the bread;
>
> The marble quarried for the arch;
> The iron become steel;
> The spoke broken from the wheel;
> The sweat of the long march;
>
> The hay-stacks cut through like loaves
> And the hundred flowers from the seed;
> All things indeed
> Though struck by the hooves
>
> Of disaster, of time due,
> Of fell loss and gain,
> All things remain,
> I can tell you, this is true.

Though burned down to stone
Though lost from the eye,
I can tell you, and not lie,—
Save of peace alone.

The imagery in some of the last poems is less specific, yet still strongly elemental; we have, I think, what Johnson called the grandeur of generality. They are timeless, impersonal in a curious way and objective—not highly idiosyncratic as so much of the best American work is. Her poems can be read and reread: they keep yielding new meanings, as all good poetry should. The ground beat of the great tradition can be heard, with the necessary subtle variations. Bogan is one of the true inheritors. Her poems create their own reality, and demand not just attention, but the emotional and spiritual response of the whole man. Such a poet will never be popular, but can and should be a true model for the young. And the best work will stay in the language as long as the language survives.

WHERE DO WE GO FROM HERE:
THE FUTURE OF FICTION

by Saul Bellow

We know that science has a future, we hope that government will have one. But it is not altogether agreed that the novel has anything but a past. There are some who say that the great novelists of the twentieth century—Proust, Joyce, Mann, and Kafka—have created sterile masterpieces, and that with them we have come to the end of the line. No further progress is possible.

It does sometimes seem that the narrative art itself has dissolved. The person, the character as we knew him in the plays of Sophocles or Shakespeare, in Cervantes, Fielding, and Balzac, has gone from us. Instead of a unitary character with his unitary personality, his ambitions, his passions, his soul, his fate, we find in modern literature an oddly dispersed, ragged, mingled, broken, amorphous creature whose outlines are everywhere, whose being is bathed in mind as the tissues are bathed in blood, and who is impossible to circumscribe in any scheme of time. A cubistic, Bergsonian, uncertain, eternal, mortal someone who shuts and opens like a concertina and makes a strange music. And what has struck artists in this century as the most amusing part of all, is that the descriptions of self that still have hold of us are made up of the old unitary foursquare traits noted according to the ancient conventions. What we insist on seeing is not a quaintly organized chaos of instinct and spirit, but what we choose to call "the personality"—a presentably combed and dressed someone who is decent, courageous, handsome, or not so handsome, but strong, or not so strong, but certainly generous, or not so generous, but anyway reliable. So it goes.

Of all modern writers, it is D. H. Lawrence who is most implacably hostile toward this convention of unitary character. For him this character of a civilized man does not really exist. What the modern civilized person calls his personality is to Lawrence figmentary: a product of civilized education, dress, manners, style, and "culture." The head of this modern personality is, he says, a wastepaper basket filled with ready-made notions. Sometimes he compares the civilized conception of character to a millstone—a painted millstone about our necks is the metaphor he makes of it. The real self, unknown, is hidden, a sunken power in us; the true identity lies deep— very deep. But we do not deal much in true identity, goes his argument. The modern character on the street, or in a conventional story or film, is what a sociologist has recently described as the "presentation" self. The attack on this presentation self or persona by modern art is a part of the war that literature, in its concern with the individual, has fought with civilization. The civilized individual is proud of his painted millstone, the burden which he believes gives him distinction. In an artist's eyes his persona is only a rude, impoverished, mass-produced figure brought into being by a civilization in need of a working force, a reservoir of personnel, a docile public that will accept suggestion and control.

The old unitary personality which still appears in popular magazine stories, in conventional best-sellers, in newspaper cartoons, and in the movies, is a figure descended from well-worn patterns, and popular art forms (like the mystery novel or the western) continue to exploit endlessly the badly faded ideas of motives and drama or love and hate. The old figures move ritualistically through the paces, finding, now and then, variations in setting and costume, but they are increasingly remote from real reality. The functions performed by these venerable literary types should be fascinating to the clinical psychologist who may be able to recognize in these stories an obsessional neurosis here, a paranoid fantasy there, or to the sociologist who sees resemblances to the organization of government bureaus or hears echoes of the modern industrial corporations. But the writer brought up in a great literary tradition not only sees these conventional stories as narcotic or brain-washing entertainments, at worst breeding strange vices, at best performing a therapeutic function. He also fears that the narrative art, which we call the novel, may have come to an end, its conception of the self exhausted and with this conception our interest in the fate of that self so conceived.

It is because of this that Gertrude Stein tells us in one of her lectures that we cannot read the great novels of the twentieth century, among which she includes her own *The Making of Americans,* for what happens next. And in fact *Ulysses, Remembrance of Things Past, The Magic Mountain,* and *The Making of Americans* do not absorb us in what happens next. They interest us in a scene, in a dialogue, a mood, an insight, in language, in character, in the revelation of a design, but they are not narratives. *Ulysses* avoids anything resembling the customary story. It is in some sense a book about literature, and offers us a history of English prose style and of the novel. It is a museum containing all the quaint armour, halberds, crossbows, and artillery pieces of literature. It exhibits them with a kind of amused irony and parodies and transcends them all. These are the things that once entranced us. Old sublimities, old dodges, old weapons, all useless now; pieces of iron once heroic, lovers' embraces once romantic, all debased by cheap exploitation, all unfit.

Language too is unfit. Erich Heller in a recent book quotes a typical observation by Hofmannsthal on the inadequacy of old forms of expression. Hofmannsthal writes, "Elements once bound together to make a world now present themselves to the poet in monstrous separateness. To speak of them coherently at all would be to speak untruthfully. The commonplace phrases of the daily round of observations seem all of a sudden insoluble riddles. The sheriff is a wicked man, the vicar is a good fellow, our neighbor must be pitied, his sons are wastrels. The baker is to be envied, his daughters are virtuous." In Hofmannsthal's *A Letter* these formulas are presented as "utterly lacking in the quality of truth." He is unable, he explains, "to see what people say and do with the simplifying eye of habit and custom. Everything falls to pieces, the pieces to pieces again, and nothing can be comprehended any more with the help of customary notions."

Character, action, and language then have been put in doubt and the Spanish philosopher Ortega y Gasset, summing up views widely held, says the novel requires a local setting with limited horizons and familiar features, traditions, occupations, classes. But as everyone knows, these old-fashioned local worlds no longer exist. Or perhaps that is inaccurate. They do exist but fail to interest the novelist. They are no longer local societies as we see them in Jane Austen or George Eliot. Our contemporary local societies have been overtaken by the world. The great cities have devoured them and now the universe itself imposes itself upon us, space with its stars comes upon us in our cities. So now we have the universe itself to face, without the comforts of community, without metaphysical certainty, without the power to distinguish the virtuous from the wicked man, surrounded by dubious realities and discovering dubious selves.

Things have collapsed about us, says D. H. Lawrence on the first page of *Lady Chatterley's Lover,* and we must each of us try to put together some sort of life. He offers us a sort of nature mysticism, love but without false romanticism, an acceptance of true desire as the first principle of recovery. Other writers have come forward with aesthetic or political or religious first principles. All the modern novelists worth mentioning aim at a point beyond customary notions, customary dramas, and customary conceptions of character. The old notion of a customary self, of the fate of an all-important Me displeases the best of them. We have lived now through innumerable successes and failures of these old selves. In American literature we have watched their progress and decline in scores of books since the Civil War, from buoyancy to depression. The Lambert Strethers, the Hurstwoods and Cowperwoods, the Gatsbys may still impress or please us as readers, but as writers, no. Their mental range is no longer adequate to these new circumstances. Those characters suit us better who stand outside society and, unlike Gatsby, have no wish to be sentimentally reconciled to it, unlike Dreiser's millionaires have no more desire for its wealth, unlike Strether are not attracted by the power of an old and knowing civilization.

This is why so many of us prefer the American novels of the nineteenth century, whose characters are very nearly removed from the civil state—*Moby Dick* and *Huckleberry Finn*. We feel in our own time that what is called the civilized condition often swings close to what Hobbes calls the state of nature, a condition of warfare, in which the life of the individual is nasty, brutish, dull and short. But we must be careful not to be swept away by the analogy. We have seen to our grief in recent European and especially German history the results of trying to bolt from all civilized and legal tradition. It is in our minds that the natural and the civil, that autarchy and discipline are most explosively mixed.

But for us here in America discipline is represented largely by the enforced repressions. We do not know much of the delights of discipline. Almost nothing of a spiritual, ennobling character is brought into the internal life of a modern American by his social institutions. He must discover it in his own experience, by his own luck as an explorer, or not at all. Society feeds him, clothes him, to an extent protects him, and he is its infant. If he accepts the state of infancy, contentment can be his. But if the idea of higher functions comes to him, he is profoundly unsettled. The hungry world is rushing on all continents toward such a contentment, and with passions and desires, frustrated since primitive times, and with the demand for justice never so loudly expressed. The danger is great that it will be satisfied with the bottles and toys of infancy. But the artist, the philosopher, the priest, the statesman are concerned with the full development of humanity—its manhood, occasionally glimpsed in our history, occasionally felt by individuals.

With all this in mind, people here and there still continue to write the sort of book we call a novel. When I am feeling blue, I can almost persuade myself that the novel, like Indian basketry, or harness-making, is a vestigial art and has no future. But we must be careful about prophecy. Even prophecy based on good historical study is a risky business, and pessimism, no less than optimism, can be made into a racket. All industrial societies have a thing about obsolescence. Classes, nations, races and cultures have in our time been declared obsolete, with results that have made ours one of the most horrible of all centuries. We must, therefore, be careful about deciding that any art is dead.

This is not a decision for a coroner's jury of critics and historians. The fact is that a great many novelists, even those who have concentrated on hate, like Céline, or on despair, like Kafka, have continued to perform a most important function. Their books have attempted, in not a few cases successfully, to create scale, to order experience, to give value, to make perspective and to carry us toward sources of life, toward life-giving things. The true believer in disorder does not like novels. He follows another calling. He is an accident lawyer, or a promoter, not a novelist. It always makes me sit up, therefore, to read yet another scolding of the modern novelist written by highly paid executives of multimillion-dollar magazines. They call upon American writers to represent the country fairly, to affirm its values, to increase its prestige in this dangerous period. Perhaps, though, novelists have a different view of what to affirm. Perhaps they are running their own sort of survey of affirmable things. They may come out against nationalism, or against the dollar, for they are an odd and unreliable lot. I have already indicated that it is the instinct of the novelist, however, to pull toward order. Now this is a pious thing to say, but I do not intend it merely to sound good. It should be understood only as the beginning of another difficulty.

What ideas of order does the novelist have and where does

he get them and what good are they in art? I have spoken of Lawrence's belief that we must put together a life for ourselves, singly, in pairs, in groups, out of the wreckage. Shipwreck and solitude are not, in his opinion, unmixed evils. They are also liberating, and if we have the strength to use our freedom we may yet stand in a true relation to nature and to other men. But how are we to reach this end? Lawrence proposes a sort of answer in *Lady Chatterley's Lover,* showing us two people alone together in the midst of a waste. I sometimes feel that *Lady Chatterley's Lover* is a sort of *Robinson Crusoe* for two, exploring man's sexual resources rather than his technical ingenuity. It is every bit as moral a novel as *Crusoe.* Connie and Mellors work at it as hard and as conscientiously as Robinson, and there are as many sermons in the one as in the other. The difference is that Lawrence aimed with all his powers at the writing of this one sort of book. To this end he shaped his life, the testing ground of his ideas. For what is the point of recommending a course of life that one has not tried oneself?

This is one way to assess the careers and achievements of many modern artists. Men like Rimbaud, Strindberg, Lawrence, Malraux, even Tolstoy, can be approached from this direction. They experiment with themselves and in some cases an artistic conclusion can come only out of the experimental results. Lawrence had no material other than what his life, that savage pilgrimage, as he called it, gave him. The ideas he tested, and tested not always by an acceptable standard, were ideas of the vital, the erotic, the instinctive. They involved us in a species of nature-mysticism which gave as a basis for morality, sexual gratification. But I am not concerned here with all the particulars of Lawrence's thesis. I am interested mainly in the connection between the understanding and the imagination, and the future place of the intelligence in imaginative literature.

At this point in a lecture this is a rather large subject to announce, but what I have in mind is relatively simple. It is necessary to admit, first, that ideas in the novel can be very dull.

There is much in modern literature, and the other arts as well, to justify our prejudice against the didactic. Opinion, said Schopenhauer, is not as valid as imagination in a work of art. One can quarrel with an opinion or judgment in a novel, but actions are beyond argument and the imagination simply accepts them. I think that many modern novels, perhaps the majority, are the result of some didactic purpose. The attempt of writers to make perspective, to make scale and to carry us toward the sources of life is, of course, the didactic intention. It involves the novelist in programs, in slogans, in political theories, religious theories, and so on. Many modern novelists seem to say to themselves, "what if," or "suppose that such and such were the case," and the results often show that the book was conceived in thought, in didactic purpose, rather than in the imagination. That is rather normal, given the state of things, the prevalence of the calculating principle in modern life, the need for conscious rules of procedure, and the generally felt need for answers. Not only books, paintings, and musical compositions, but love affairs, marriages, and even religious convictions often originate in an idea. So that the *idea* of love is more common than love, and the *idea* of belief is more often met with than faith. Some of our most respected novels have a purely mental inspiration. The results are sometimes very pleasing because they can so easily be discussed, but the ideas in them generally have more substance than the characters who hold them.

American literature in the nineteenth century was highly didactic. Emerson, Thoreau, Whitman, and even Melville were didactic writers. They wished to instruct a young and raw nation. American literature in the twentieth century has remained didactic, but it has also been unintellectual. This is not to say that thought is lacking in the twentieth-century American novel, but it exists under strange handicaps and is much disguised. In *A Farewell to Arms* Hemingway makes a list of subjects we must no longer speak about—a catalogue of polluted words, words which have been ruined by the rhetoric of criminal politicians and misleaders. Then Hemingway, and we must respect him for it, attempts to represent these betrayed qualities without using the words themselves. Thus we have courage without the word, honor without the word, and in *The Old Man and the Sea* we are offered a sort of Christian endurance, also without specific terms. Carried to this length, the attempt to represent ideas while sternly forbidding thought begins to look like a curious and highly sophisticated game. It shows a great skepticism of the strength of art. It makes it appear as though ideas openly expressed would be too much for art to bear.

We have developed in American fiction a strange combination of extreme naïveté in the characters and of profundity implicit in the writing, in the techniques themselves and in the language, but the language of thought itself is banned, it is considered dangerous and destructive. American writers appear to have a strong loyalty to the people, to the common man; perhaps in some cases the word for this is not loyalty, perhaps it might better be described as *fear*. But a writer should aim to reach all levels of society and as many levels of thought as possible, avoiding democratic prejudice as much as intellectual snobbery. Why should he be ashamed of thinking? I do not claim that all writers can think, or should think. Some are peculiarly inept at ideas and we would harm them by insisting that they philosophize. But the records show that most artists are intellectually active, and it is only now in a world increasingly intellectualized, more and more dominated by the productions of scientific thought, that they seem strangely reluctant to use their brains or to give any sign that they have brains to use.

All through the nineteenth century the conviction increases in novelists as different as Goncharov in Russia and Thomas Hardy in England that thought is linked with passivity and is devitalizing. And in the masterpieces of the twentieth century the thinker usually has a weak grip on life. But by now an alternative, passionate activity without ideas, has also been well explored in novels of adventure, hunting, combat, and eroticism. Meanwhile, miracles, born of thought, have been largely ignored by modern literature. If narration is neglected by novelists like Proust and Joyce, the reasons are that for a time the drama has passed from external action to internal movement. In Proust and Joyce we are enclosed by and held within a single consciousness. In this inner realm the writer's art dominates everything. The drama has left external action because the old ways of describing interests, of describing the fate of the individual, have lost their power. Is the sheriff a good fellow? Is our neighbor to be pitied? Are the baker's daughters virtuous? We see such questions now as belonging to a dead system, mere formulas. It is possible that our hearts would open again to the baker's daughters if we understood them differently.

A clue may be offered by Pascal, who said there are no dull people, only dull points of view. Maybe that is going a little far. (A religious philosophy is bound to maintain that every soul is infinitely precious and, therefore, infinitely interesting.) But it begins perhaps to be evident what my position is. Imagination, binding itself to dull viewpoints, puts an end to stories. The imagination is looking for new ways to express virtue. American society just now is in the grip of certain common falsehoods about virtue—not that anyone really believes them. And these cheerful falsehoods beget their opposites in fiction, a dark literature, a literature of victimization, of old people sitting in ash cans waiting for the breath of life to depart. This is the way things stand; only this remains to be added, that we have barely begun to comprehend what a human being is, and that the baker's daughters may have revelations and miracles to offer to keep fascinated novelists busy until the end of time.

I would like to add this also, in conclusion, about good thought and bad thought in the novel. In a way it doesn't matter what sort of line the novelist is pushing, what he is affirming. If he has nothing to offer but his didactic purpose he is a bad writer. His ideas have ruined him. He could not afford the expense of maintaining them. It is not the didactic purpose itself which is a bad thing, and the modern novelist drawing back from the dangers of didacticism has often become strangely unreal, and the purity of his belief in art for art in some cases has been peculiarly unattractive. Among modern novelists the bravest have taken the risk of teaching and have not been afraid of using the terms of religion, science, philosophy, and politics. Only they have been prepared to admit the strongest possible arguments against their own positions.

Here we see the difference between a didactic novelist like D. H. Lawrence and one like Dostoevski. When he was writing *The Brothers Karamazov* and had just ended the famous conversation between Ivan and Alyosha, in which Ivan, despair- of justice, offers to return his ticket to God, Dostoevski wrote to one of his correspondents that he must now attempt, through Father Zossima, to answer Ivan's arguments. But he has in advance all but devastated his own position. This, I think, is the greatest achievement possible in a novel of ideas. It becomes art when the views most opposite to the author's own are allowed to exist in full strength. Without this a novel of ideas is mere self-indulgence, and didacticism is simply axe-grinding. The opposites must be free to range themselves against each other, and they must be passionately expressed on both sides. It is for this reason that I say it doesn't matter much what the writer's personal position is, what he wishes to affirm. He may affirm principles we all approve of and write very bad novels.

The novel, to recover and to flourish, requires new ideas about humankind. These ideas in turn cannot live in themselves. Merely asserted, they show nothing but the good will of the author. They must therefore be discovered and not invented. We must see them in flesh and blood. There would be no point in continuing at all if many writers did not feel the existence of these unrecognized qualities. They are present and they demand release and expression.

THE BURDENS OF BIOGRAPHY

by Mark Schorer

Many of you know the anecdote about Samuel Johnson and James Boswell in which Boswell, with his obsessive concern for the accumulation of more and more details of Johnson's life and character, was questioning a third person about Johnson in Johnson's presence, when Johnson suddenly thundered at him, "You have but two subjects, yourself and me. I am sick of both."

Let this anecdote serve as my text, and in a more special way than the exasperated Dr. Johnson intended, namely, that biography itself has two subjects, and two subjects only—the figure whose life is being recreated, of course, and the mind that is recreating it, the scrutinizing biographer no less than the object of his scrutiny. Let me use it, too, to suggest that the largest burdens of biography are twofold: one, of course, on the man who has undertaken the work, responsibilities much more subtle than may at first appear and conceivably so enervating that he may well be tempted to throw up his hands and shout, "I'm sick of it"; the other on the ghost of the man who is not to be permitted the decent obscurity of death and who, seeing how he is being made to live, might well, had he a voice, shout, "I am sick of both!" And let me use this anecdote finally as a kind of warning, even as a request for forgiveness of what may well seem to be an exercise in egocentricity that goes far beyond Boswellian vanity. For I must be personal if I am to speak on this subject at all.

I spent some years in research for a biography and some more

147

years in writing what proved to be a rather large book. I had not intended to speak directly about that book or of my experience in writing it. I had hoped to speak generally on biography as an art. I had written a biography but I had never read much about the nature of biography or how to write it. In preparation—as I thought—I have read a half dozen books, or more, on this subject, and I regret to say that I learned very little. It is difficult, but not impossible, to set up a definition of the novel more precise than E. M. Forster's quotation from the Frenchman, Chevalley, that a novel is "a fiction in prose of a certain extent." It is even more difficult to define biography, so various is it, or to set up rules for its composition, although this has been attempted. I am forced, for this reason, chiefly to posing some questions and then to answering them as well as I can from my own experience.

A writer of fiction, turning to biography, discovers the difference immediately (later, he will discover the similarities as well); as a writer of fiction he was a free man; as a biographer, he is writing in chains, as it were. As a writer of fiction, he invented his subject, even when he modeled it on real events and real people, and was free to handle it as he pleased; as a biographer, he is given his subject and is obliged to stay rigorously with its facts. This is, of course, a burden, but often, one discovers, a burden that it is a pleasure to carry. For facts can be surprisingly friendly, and they have, not infrequently, an eloquence, even a kind of poetry, that may well go far beyond the inventions of imagination.

I had thought, as I came to the end of my biography, that I would next write a short novel—a novel about Sinclair Lewis, no less, in which I could do some telescoping and some embroidering which the limits of biography did not allow, and also in which, with the happy disguises of fiction, I could use some episodes that my at least rudimentary sense of the power of legal restraints had not allowed. I gave up that idea. Almost simultaneously with the publication of my biography, a novel about Sinclair Lewis was published. It provided a sharply drawn picture of some of Lewis's most striking characteristics, but in its invented elements—chiefly, its plot—it did not do so well. It is known that toward the end of his life Lewis enjoyed the company of a young actress as his mistress. She was a few years younger than the older of Lewis's two sons, and in real life Lewis would try to amuse her with the company of people of her own age, including this son. But when now and then he urged the young man to take her out for an evening, to dinner or to the films, he complained to his mother: "I don't want to take her out. She bores me." In the novel I have in mind, the aging novelist's son falls in love with the young woman, and when in the climax of the story the father discovers the affair his world at last crashes into total ruin. But the facts, while less melodramatic, were much more interesting, certainly more macabre. After the young woman left Lewis to marry a man of roughly her age, Lewis decided to go abroad; but he wanted a companion, and he invited a number of old friends and a number of near strangers to travel with him. All refused. Then he turned to the young woman's mother, a plain, inarticulate, simple New Jersey housewife, who accepted. And Lewis, with his extraordinary gift for self-deception, wrote back to his friends to say how graciously the Florentines were receiving her. "Donna Caterina," they called her, he said. But in the obituary columns of at least one Florentine newspaper, she was referred to as *una vecchia gouvernante*—an old governess. Here I am happy to be confined to the pathos of fact.

Let me give you another and a much briefer illustration of what I have called the friendliness of facts. Lewis died of what we would call a heart attack; but in the official records of the Roman hospital in which he died, the cause of his death is given in another terminology, presumably a commonplace in the vocabulary of Italian medicine: *paralisi cardiaca*. Could I possibly have invented it? Paralysis of the heart. This, in its metaphorical significance, I had long before discovered was the very theme of Lewis's life and a major theme of the whole book: his incapacity for love. Is this not poetry? and more than that, magnificently, poetic justice?

There is then, first of all, the body of fact about one's subject. These details, if one is a responsible biographer, one accumulates with all the hoarding assiduity of a Boswell, the most trivial along with the most striking. One *must* accumulate them all, or as many of them as can be retrieved from mouldering documents, for until one is in possession of them all, one does not know two important things: one, what the book is to be about; and two, what shape the book will have. It is probable, however, that about halfway through the process of accumulation one begins to have some sense of each of these matters, since the accumulation is not made according to chronology but in a hit or miss fashion as one picks up scrap after scrap at whatever point it is offered. (For my book, for example, my earliest extensive researches, because I happened to be living in Italy when I began, were with the end of the Lewis life.) Italy, except for some newspaper accounts, did not provide much by way of documents, but it contained the places where he lived—his Florentine house, his last, gave me more eloquent facts than scores of documents could have—and it contained besides a host of living witnesses.

When one is writing the life of a person only recently dead, living witnesses are, of course, an essential source of information. And one discovers all too soon the burden that such evidence entails. Sometimes I wished that I had ten years more, for in that time most of those people would have gone away and I would no longer be confused by their conflicting tales and would in fact be free to say what I wished about *them*. Quite as often I despaired when, just as I was about to get to an important informant, he *did* suddenly go away.

The first problem with living witnesses is simply human vanity. It is natural enough that anyone who knows that he is to appear in a book will wish to appear to the best advantage. Inevitably, then, he will do one of two things, or both, when he talks to the biographer: he will be exasperatingly reticent or he will dress up the circumstances. Then there are those who wish to be memorialized as having had a more important association with the subject than the facts will support. Fortunate-ly, if one has enough living witnesses, one can generally check the accuracy of one against the testimony of another or of others. And often, of course, a letter, a scrap of entry in a diary or a journal, a casual item in a newspaper, a published reminiscence will turn up to provide the control for which one is looking. This is not to say, of course, that documents in themselves are to be trusted simply because they are documents, even of the most personal kind. Leon Edel, the biographer of Henry James, who has read some seven thousand letters by James, tells us of the analytical scouring he must do to get beyond the "mere twaddle of graciousness" to the trustworthy kernel, if it is there at all. And Sinclair Lewis, after he was famous but still writing his aged father faithful weekly letters, mainly from Europe, enjoined his young nephew, who read these letters with adolescent fascination, not to take them very seriously, that he wrote his father only what his father wanted to hear. So documents, too, must be checked against other documents, and back against that talk from personal witnesses that may or may not represent the truth.

A third kind of difficulty presented by living witnesses evidences itself immediately when one is dealing with a personality like Sinclair Lewis's—at once so extreme in gregariousness and so short in patience. The number of associates that resulted from the first quality proposed an almost endless round of interviews which I finally ended rather arbitrarily, but I am not thinking of that problem so much as I am of the hurt feelings that resulted from the second quality. Lewis was like Richard Savage in at least one item in Johnson's life of that unhappy man:

> It was his peculiar happiness, that he scarcely ever found a stranger whom he did not leave a friend; but it must likewise be added that he had not often a friend long, without obliging him to become a stranger.

Hurt feelings lingering, even festering over the years, do not

make for highly reliable testimony. One tends to come away
with only the anger, the rancor, the wound—and beyond a
certain point, these are not of much use to the biographer.

A more serious difficulty with living witnesses is the simple
fallibility of human memory. I have told this anecdote before,
but let me tell it again, because the general principle involved
has again been amusingly illustrated, for me, since the publication of my book. Biography, as Bernard de Voto wrote, "is not
concerned with the *must* but only with the *did*." Yet one soon
finds, when writing the life of a man who gained great public
prominence, that in many minds certain things *must* have happened even if they *did* not. A prominent man is, in many ways,
a mythological man.

If Sinclair Lewis became the most famous man ever to
have grown up in Sauk Centre, Minnesota, his youth there
must have held the evidence, even if it was only belatedly observed. Thus, one of my witnesses, a contemporary of my subject, told me how, in June of 1902, graduating from the Sauk
Centre High School in a class of seven, Sinclair Lewis, that
baffled, awkward boy of seventeen, gave a brilliant valedictory
address on the subject of "The Westward March of Empire."
The subject was appropriate enough to the time, but the
address itself was not appropriate to the academic circumstances
of Harry Lewis. In this detail, the documentary control was
easy enough to come by: the local newspaper under the proper
date, which summarized the famous address and demonstrated quite clearly that it had been delivered, not by my
subject, but by my informant himself. There is touching humil-
ity in this anecdote, but I fear only a rudimentary sense of
history. On his graduation from a high school with a class that
had three places of honor open to it, Sinclair Lewis was, for a
change, completely silent.

This curious experience came back to my mind a few
months ago when I had a letter of congratulation from my
high-school English teacher in my sophomore year in the Sauk
City (Wisconsin) High School—named after the same Indian
tribe, an almost interchangeable town with Sauk Centre, Min-

nesota, but, it happens, a different one. She was writing to congratulate me. She always knew that some day I would be famous. (Let me say quickly that this is only *her* view.) She supposed that I would not remember her (of course, I do; did she not dismiss me from class for snickering about a word in *Macbeth* for which Sauk City preferred a euphemism?) She was always, she said, afraid of me, because she felt that I knew so much more about the subject that she did, and that I would expose her ignorance. I was the "brightest boy in the school."

Ha! My academic record in Sauk City is no doubt quite as available as was Sinclair Lewis' in Sauk Centre, but I have no wish to examine it. I know what it was—highly undistinguished And so was all my academic work until I was well into graduate study. My undergraduate record, today, would not admit me to any self-respecting graduate school, certainly not that of Michigan, probably not that of Harvard, where, as gawky as Sinclair Lewis at Yale, I mysteriously went.

This is all parenthesis, but not, I hope to indicate before I finish, as gratuitously parenthetical as it may now appear. And it leads me to the next point that I would like to raise; who is the best biographer for a given subject?

Of all the living witnesses whom I approached, only four declined to be of help. Two of these were men who had known Lewis intimately and planned to write biographical memoirs of their own; naturally, they did not wish to share their material with me. A third was a man who had known Lewis during a very large part of his life, had been Lewis's editor for many years, but unfortunately, was also the editor of one of those first two men who planned to write his own Lewis biography; naturally, his interests were with that book, not with mine. The fourth was Lewis's last secretary, the man with whom Lewis was living at the time of his death, the man who, in the last years in Europe, managed his affairs. His refusal to see me, made on the telephone in Rome, remains a mystery to me; but I am grateful to him, for his refusal also enabled me to make something of a mystery of him. Since he would not see me,

I had to depend upon the only available evidence for that association—hearsay. Much of it came from interesting sources—Bernard Berenson, for example, who declared to me, "I know a minor Central European adventurer when I see one." It is only in this part of the book, I believe, the very end, and only because of the lacuna which the obdurate ex-secretary provided, that my fictional impulses necessarily came into play. They made for a nice bit of implied melodrama and, I believe, for truth of its own kind as well. And for once I was freed of the vexatious business of trying to force an informant to be truthful!

Now it is possible that those two men who had known Lewis over a number of years, or even his editor, would have written better biographies than mine. Samuel Johnson would have thought so. The best biography, in his view, is written by the subject himself; in other words, the best biography is autobiography. Had Johnson had the interest to write his autobiography, it would, I suspect, have been brief and incisive and honest and masterly; but we can be certain that it would not have given us that full-bodied portrait that the patient drudgery of Boswell created in the great masterpiece of all English biography. In the degree to which it would have been shorter it would have been less true. Johnson was a man of unusual self-knowledge, but he was also a man of unusual reticence. Boswell's very naïveté gave him an advantage; so did his habit of garrulousness. And Johnson, we should remind ourselves, was an exceptional man, fearful of a number of things but never of contemplating his own nature. Most men are. Certainly my subject was. He wrote many autobiographical sketches, and all of them are inaccurate and untrustworthy, deliberate softenings of what was harsh, deliberate alterations of fact for the sake of entertainment, confusions of fact, obfuscations—all in need of correction. One of my informants has told me that, toward the end of his life, Lewis spent many hours, usually in drunken rages, dictating fragments of his autobiography to her, all later to be assembled in a book. I have not been permitted to see her notes, if they exist, and until

I am, I shall permit myself to doubt that they exist. Nothing in Sinclair Lewis's writings suggests that he could have been his own biographer.

I shall have something to say presently about the uses to which a writer's own works can be put by his biographer. At this point I wish only to point out the hazards. With a writer such as Sinclair Lewis, so little inclined toward candor with himself, it would be fatal to take with any literalness those fictional passages of his that do seem to arise from his immediate experience. Like Richard Savage, to whom I shall come in a moment, Lewis had mistaken preconceptions about the simple life but no gift for living it, yet he always yearned for a wilderness excursion. When his brother finally made such a trip into Saskatchewan possible, it began, for Lewis, as a series of drunken adventures and ended as a number of days so acutely uncomfortable that he abandoned the trip before it was half over and headed back for civilization. When he came to use the experience in fiction—in a melodramatic novel called *Mantrap* —the figure who corresponds to Lewis is the heroic and vindicated city man in the wilderness, and the novel provided a suitable film script for the talents of Clara Bow. In *Dodsworth,* which has commonly been read as an account of the decay of Lewis's first marriage, nothing can be trusted but the *feelings* of the hero for his first wife, and his *feelings* for the woman who was to become his second. But feelings are not precisely biographical fact. Alcohol was a grave problem for Lewis, who on untold occasions suffered the horrors of hangover and the acute pangs of guilt that go with that condition; but he almost never wrote about these matters. In one foolish story he began to, but soon turned the truly reported details into the mechanics of a tricky plot directed toward the kind of "happy ending" that he himself was never to know. Never trust the author, said D. H. Lawrence. Trust the tale. Do not, he meant, believe the author when he lectures us; believe only the conduct of the narrative itself, and the resolution of its values. If we follow this sound advice with Sinclair Lewis, we arrive at one conclusion: self-deception.

After the subject himself, the best biographer was, Johnson thought, a close friend, a man who had seen his subject in the most intimate circumstances of his life over a long period, who knew the accents of his talk, who knew his physical habits, the way he walked, the way he behaved at table, the way he laughed, the degree to which he permitted his sorrows to show. Again, one can only wonder.

Johnson himself, when he came to write the life of his friend, Richard Savage, produced a work of art—he could not do less; but did he, in a strict sense, produce a proper biography of Richard Savage? Had he known Savage less intimately, might he not have paused to question Savage's own account of his birth and upbringing, found his friend not the innocent victim of monstrous abuses but an unsuccessful fraud, found his friend's supposed mother not the implausible fiend who has come down to us through the *Life,* but an indiscreet woman unsuccessfully put upon by a small villain? Recent scholarship suggests such miscalculations in Johnson's narrative, and so, indeed, does the narrative itself on any close inspection. Even Boswell, that glorious simpleton, had his doubts about this much of the narrative. And it is all the more surprising in that, at other points, Johnson could estimate his friend so ably. With what lovely irony he writes when he tells us how Savage's friends, eager to remove him from the threats of his debtors, arrange to ship him off to the wilds of Wales. Savage, London-born and bred, familiar only with the city, low life, and literature, had certain preconceptions about the country that Johnson was perfectly capable of defining and enjoying:

> . . . he had planned out a scheme of life for the country, of which he had no knowledge but from pastorals and songs. He imagined that he should be transported to scenes of flowery felicity, like those which one poet has reflected to another; and had projected a perpetual round of inno-

cent pleasures, of which he suspected no interruption from pride, or ignorance, or brutality.

With these expectations he was so enchanted, that when he was once gently reproached by a friend for submitting to live upon a subscription, and advised rather by a resolute exertion of his abilities to support himself, he could not bear to debar himself from the happiness which was to be found in the calm of a cottage, or lose the opportunity of listening, without intermission, to the melody of the nightingale, which he believed was to be heard from every bramble, and which he did not fail to mention as a very important part of the happiness of a country life.

And yet, in spite of such perspicacity, the whole may very well be based on a miscalculation for the very reason that these men were intimates, had loved one another too much in life, too little, perhaps, in the imagination. There are deeper forms of intimacy than friendship.

Personal intimacy with one's subject would certainly have those advantages for the biographer that Johnson names, but does it not have certain disadvantages, too, and perhaps larger ones? Personal intimacy can readily lead to panegyric, which is not biography, for there are obligations to friendship even after one's friend is dead. Inversely, if hurt feelings are involved, it can lead to self-protective distortions and omissions, which are the chief faults of the first Mrs. Lewis's *roman à clef*, *Half a Loaf*, and her more recent biography of Lewis, *With Love from Gracie*. Personal intimacy, more significantly, may lead to mere memoir, which again is not proper biography, books of the "I Knew Him When" variety, or at least may permit intrusions of personal reminiscence which, if they do not decree the total shape, may yet throw the whole off balance (the only flaw in Andrew Turnbull's otherwise beautiful life of Scott Fitzgerald).

There is a further limitation: an intimate friend would almost certainly feel that he knew his subject to start with and conclude that much plain drudgery in accumulating all that detail, which a more impersonal biographer regards as essential to his enterprise, was not essential at all. For, believe me, the first thing that a biographer must be is a drudge. I wonder if either of those two men—one old and tired, the other a very busy and highly successful foreign correspondent—would, for example, have been willing to read through (and take the full notes which are routine for a trained scholar) Lewis's twenty-one novels, all but five of them of small literary worth and some of them almost unbelievably poor, let alone track down in any number of different libraries the hundred-odd stories, almost all of them worse than poor, which Lewis published in the highly paying but also highly ephemeral national periodicals of large circulation. I cannot believe it. And yet I do believe, with Professor Pottle, that among the obligations of a man who proposes to write a *literary* biography one of the first is to read through the complete works of his subject. And I will add a point that Professor Pottle does not, I think, make: that he will find that much of them he will have to read a second time, and some a third and a fourth.

And all this for extra-literary purposes, for reasons that have little to do with the literary worth of his subject's works. I do not mean to suggest that a literary biographer is not expected to deliver a literary judgment, indeed, a whole series of them; of course he is, that is his ultimate obligation. But even if the works are treated mainly as biographical events (as I chose, on the whole, to treat Lewis's) they must be read and analyzed, for in some important ways they are the clue to and even the chart of the mind and being of his subject. This is particularly the situation if the work is imaginative, and even if it is not generally autobiographical in the usual sense (and Lewis's certainly was not), it is nevertheless an autobiography of the spirit. Its lineaments are to be detected in the situations and the themes that recur, in repeated and developing images, in certain character types that seem to haunt the author. Almost all of Sinclair Lewis's works, one discovers after a time, are built on the same general idea, of a character who is trying to escape from something restrictive into some kind of freedom. In the novels, the restrictions—convention, hypocrisy, injustice, institutions, et cetera—are metaphors, one finds at last, for a restriction that was unutterable for him in his life. For the second large theme of that life is Lewis's own frenetic and endless and impossible attempt to escape from the restrictions of his self into a freedom that does not exist.

We have gone beyond the drudge, who must accumulate, to the critic, who must analyze, and who is perceptive enough to see what is basically *there* in the work. The drudge alone could compile his material into a chronological catalogue, even a chronicle of sorts; but that is not proper biography. The critic alone, if he can see not only what is basically there in the work, but also how it threads its way through the whole mass of accumulated detail, will have moved toward the formal skeleton of a biography; but that is not yet proper biography either. No, now we need a third man, and you must forgive me for saying that he must be an artist, not only the man who can bring shape out of the mass but more especially the man who can give it living shape; and I do not mean only that he must make his subject live, but also that he must make him live in the reanimated history of his time, make him live in a living world. And now that we have come to the most interesting point, I too have reached the unutterable, the burden that is ineffable: I do not know how it is done. I can only hope that in some small way, perhaps, I did it.

We can talk about the shape if not about its animation. This brings us to the similarities with fiction, for biography, also, is a narrative art, and it seems probable that all the principles that pertain to fiction except for one—the free exercise of invention—pertain to proper biography. A novelist has his whole world of experience, real and imaginary, to draw from; how does he carve out of that limitless and undifferentiated mass the materials that fall into pattern in his beautiful, autonomous units? He has, of course, for each work, a theme, and his theme deter-

mines his selection of detail. The biographer finds his themes
—the strains that seem most persistently to recur—in that mass
of accumulated detail and selects from the mass accordingly.
I am aware that some of my readers do not think that I selected
drastically enough and others think that I did not select at all;
the fact is that I did not, for example, report on every drunken
rumpus, as one reviewer has complained, but only on, I suppose, some six or ten of them, whereas there must have been
at least ten times ten and possibly one hundred times six of
them. But if from my mention of six or ten, my exhausted
reader has some sense of the exhausting intemperance to which
Sinclair Lewis, in long stretches of his life, was addicted, I am
at least partially vindicated: the reader, who carries the least
burden, except perhaps on his pocketbook, has at least been
made to suffer with my subject and with me. And while we
are on intemperance and the problem of selection from the
whole possible body of detail, may I remind you that it was
only as recently as 1903, the year after Sinclair Lewis's inaus-
picious graduation from high school, that Sir Edmund Gosse
arrived at the conclusion that the one horrendous fact about
his subject which a biographer should under no circumstances
reveal is his addiction to drink. If we were today to eliminate
this phenomenon, what would the biographers of American
writers have to write about?

For several centuries "the ethics of biography (as Sir Edmund entitled his essay of 1903) was the subject of much discussion: what, in any body of accumulated detail, was clearly
inadmissible by the biographer? Gibbon, in the eighteenth
century, thought that everything was admissible, and so did
Johnson except for one occasion when he reversed himself
and opined that it was better to repress a detail than hurt the
feelings of "a widow, a daughter, a brother, or a friend." In
the nineteenth century, while biographies grew longer and
longer, they tended to revert to their origins in England and
become mere works of hagiography. Today, I believe, the
problem of selection is not made more acute by what were once
thought of as ethical considerations. One should write in any-

thing that is true and relevant to one's themes—anything, that is, that will not bring us into court. In this sense, at least, therefore, the biographer today enjoys some of the freedom of the novelist, and he does not have to publish that famous and foolish disclaimer at the front of his book about how nothing in it has any relation whatever to any real person, now living or now dead.

Assume that our biographer has his several themes, those tensions or preoccupations or behavioral patterns that occur most frequently in the mass of the life, and that he can select his details accordingly. Like the novelist he faces a second step. All those themes must somehow be unified, the biographer, like the novelist, must find an appropriate emphasis, or general meaning. When I was about midway in my research, I decided that I would try to summarize Lewis's biography in a subtitle: *An American Life*. I had in mind at least a dozen things, not really separate but separable. I can mention a few. I saw Lewis's life, for instance, as representative of the curious social mobility of American life in general—the poor beginnings and the sudden, fantastic, uneasy success. I saw it more specifically as an extreme example of the fate of so many American writers—the quick supremacy and the long, dreary decline joined with an equally dreary debauchery. I began to see Lewis's life as peculiarly American in the very ambiguities that tore it apart—his love for his country, sometimes nearly chauvinistic, and his unhappy dislike of much of it. I might have borrowed a subtitle from Melville and called it *Sinclair Lewis: The Ambiguities*. Or *The Paradoxes*. For the very ambiguities of American life, those paradoxical polarities of an individualistic society which destroys individuality, an affluent society which does not permit millions of its citizens the merest decencies, a peace-living society which does best in a wartime economy—all those ambiguities that engendered Lewis's ambiguous feelings about his country are also represented in the profoundest ambiguities of his own character. And now perhaps you can see how the biographer, subjective being, enters the objective facts. For clearly I am talking like a novelist, talking about America as it seems to me, and finding in the objective materials of a single life facts that will support that view.

We have, then, some themes and what is meant to be a unifying attitude. We must have, beyond these, a general shape, or form, or rhythm—again, like the novel. Themes and attitude, taking always into account the general chronology of real events which in large part determined them, will in turn determine this. The shape of my book seemed fairly obvious long before I was into it very deeply—a general pattern of rise, climax, and frenzied fall, containing within it many lesser patterns of rise-climax-fall, a few of them large. And like the novelist, the biographer needs still another element; he needs a plot, an element of persistent conflict that will animate not only the subject himself but that pattern which his life enacts, over and over in little, and once and once only in the whole that it was. Here the facts of Lewis's life were most obliging, and the central conflict (highlighted, of course, by my own view of things) seemed clear enough; first the quarrel of his environment with him, then his quarrel with his environment, and that quarrel turning very early but with slowly increasing intensity into his quarrel with himself and his attempt to escape it, to escape the self.

I begin to sound like an amateur psychologist and for that I am sorry, since I tried very hard in my book to avoid precisely that. A biographer, like any other civilized man, should know about the developments of modern psychology, but I do not think that he should write as if he were indeed a psychoanalyst. Some of my reviewers wished that I had; they wished that at some point I had said plainly, flatly, what was *wrong* with Sinclair Lewis. It was precisely because I was unwilling to make such a statement that I made the book so long. I wanted to give the reader all the evidence that I coherently could which would permit him to say to himself what was wrong with Sinclair Lewis. But more than that, I wanted him to believe that Sinclair Lewis was a living man, and I wanted him to be moved by his life. I do not think that the jargon of psycho-analysis would have heightened either the comedy or the pathos of that life. A friend of mine, a psychoanalyst, has recently sent me a paper of hers on a phenomenon that she has observed and calls "the Pollyanna Paranoid." This is the person who conceives of an impossibly beautiful future which, when it does not develop, as it cannot, permits him to feel betrayed and persecuted. The concept can explain a good deal about Sinclair Lewis, if not everything. But I insist that the term would hardly have improved my prose.

And this is the final matter that I must touch upon, and probably the most important. Thomas Carlyle, I believe, said that a well-written life is a much rarer thing than a well-spent one. I do not know if my life of Lewis is well-written, but I do know that I gave as much thought as a novelist does to the kind of prose that would be most appropriate to that subject, to the tone that my prose would strike. Recently I was invited to attempt now a biography of Stephen Crane, and while I have still a good deal to learn about Crane's life (and hence of my relation to that subject) I know most of his writing, and already I am wondering what tone will be most appropriate to that subject. (I am thinking about something that I call to myself *"athletic* elegance.") But for the life of Sinclair Lewis, I decided, lived with so little dignity and so much fret and fury, and, on the literary side, producing so much loose and garrulous bulk, the tone must be casual—never exalted, seldom formal, but rather conversational, perhaps rambling a bit, frequently ironical, now and then a little snide. I wanted the reader to feel that I was talking to him, or as if he were overhearing me as I talked to Sinclair Lewis, saying in effect over and over, You did that . . . it was funny, wasn't it . . . how did it go again? . . . why?

It was only after I was well into the book, accustomed to that tone—or whatever tone it was that I achieved—that I began to wonder about my relationship to Sinclair Lewis and to begin to understand how much of that relationship was making the substance of the book. Not the facts; they were there. Not the themes; they were there. Not even the plot; that was there. But the general attitude, the whole coloration, because that was I, or rather, the two of us together. Here we can differentiate between what goes into fiction (*I*, really), and into history (*they*, really), and into biography (he *and* I). For is not biography, when we reduce it to its essential nature, simply—or complexly—the interpenetration of one mind by another, and is this not, for all the apparent objectivity one may achieve, a considerably subjective operation? "History," said the great Theodor Mommsen, "is neither written nor made without love or hate." He could have made that observation even more appropriately of biography. In my relationship with Lewis, as I began to scrutinize it and as it was revealing itself in my tone, there were both love and hate, and there were also pity, shame, much impatience. There were also self-love and self-hate and self-pity, and the shame and the impatience were as much for myself as for him.

Why did I—first of all—and now we are at what is really the beginning—why did I choose to write this life? It is true that I was invited to write it, but surely I could have said no. I believe now that from the outset I was challenged by what I unconsciously felt to be a strange affinity, an affinity perhaps only demonstrated by the fact that my literary tastes, as they matured, had moved about as far away from his as is possible. There was, of course, the obvious affinity of our beginnings—the same kind of raw small Midwestern towns, probably much the same kind of inept and unsuccessful boys in that particular man's world. But I discovered many more, and many that were more subtle. Should I try to spell them out now I would be writing my autobiography, or even confession, and I have no such inclination. But I can give you a hint or two: all the careless writing, all the ill-conceived ambitions, all the bad manners, all the irrational fits of temper, all the excesses of conduct, all the immature, lifelong frivolities and regrettable follies. That is a little of it. There is much more. And those of my critics who have complained of an imputed lack of sympathy with my subject might have said with equal accuracy and greater justice, with sharper perception certainly, and probably with more kindness, that I had refused to be self-indulgent.

Perhaps this is where the psychoanalyst is really needed—not in the biographer analyzing his subject, but beyond both of them, analyzing their symbiotic relationship. And it is perhaps this relationship that explains why one of those critics who complained of my want of sympathy—Mr. Irving Howe—found the book paradoxically moving, in spite of all my icy refusal to be moved.

Critics are not as wise as they sometimes sound and never as wise as they believe. I speak now as a critic, and a self-critic. My long conversation with Sinclair Lewis—my nine years' captivity with him, one witty journalist called it—taught me a good deal. As I learned about him with all his stubborn deficiency in self-knowledge, I believe that I gained in self-knowledge. I am not a better man, certainly, for having written his life; but I think that I am a wiser one. And I can only hope that my gratitude to him for that will lighten a little the onus of the life with which I have burdened him.

ON RECOGNITION

by Arthur Miller

I accepted the Hopwood Committee's invitation to speak today with misgivings. In fact, many years ago I swore that if I were ever asked to, I would never speak on the occasion of the award ceremonies. This, because I recalled too vividly how I sat where you are sitting now, listening to I think it was Christopher Morley droning on and on in what was probably a fascinating way, while on the table were the envelopes with the winners' names inside. If there was ever a captive audience, this is it. You have to listen to me or you don't get your money, and who knows, I could go on for an hour. It is even worse when I know that the very people I am most interested in reaching—namely the best writers among you and presumably the ones who are going to win today—are least likely to be paying me any attention.

So in the hope of flagging down your greedily racing thoughts, I am going to speak today on a subject which, along with money, must surely be on your minds. On Recognition. It may not sound like a particularly literary subject, but you would be amazed at how powerful a force it is in literary affairs. Offhand, I should say that if everybody who expressed a desire to be a writer were automatically recognized and were given a lapel button saying "Writer," approximately eighty per cent of those who devote their lives to some form of writing or another would not have bothered. I can even imagine a society in which practically everybody is born a writer, and there is a contest each year in some university where prizes are given for the most persuasive *business proposition*. I can imagine the

winners' parents going around boasting, "Imagine, my son won
a prize for not writing!" I can imagine the genius business man
in such a society surrounded after his lecture by envious people
all asking the same questions—"How did you start? What is it
like not to be stuck at home every day, having to write a poem
or a play like everybody else, but to go off by yourself into
a nice busy office where all you've got to deal with are other
people?"

It's hard, but I can imagine it. Distinction, after all, is
relative. More precisely, distinction abhors relatives. In some
cases it despises just about everybody. The other day I got a
pamphlet containing three speeches by writers delivered at the
Library of Congress under some grant or other, and one of
them, McKinlay Kantor's, I may as well say, was almost
wholly taken up with an attack on other historical novelists
who fail to do enough research to justify the honor of being
called an historical novelist. It turns out that Lincoln did not
have a deep baritone, as some writer had written in a recent
best-seller, but a high nasal twang, and that the belt-buckle
worn by Union soldiers did not say U.S.A. on it but U.S. He
was also mad at Stephen Crane because the *Red Badge of
Courage* could have been about any war and was not specifically what it claimed, a book about the Civil War. In short,
distinction in itself is no guarantee of anything in particular.

The trouble is that the writer has to win recognition almost
before he is recognizable. Before, that is, he is distinct. He needs
recognition in order to win it. He therefore has to invent it first
in the hope that his invention will be pronounced a fact by
the outside world. The effort to first invent one's own distinction, and then to get others to agree to it, is so strenuous
that in a great many cases the man is exhausted just when
he ought to be starting. But having won his own reality, so
to speak, having won his public license to practice his recognition, he faces the danger—possibly the greatest danger writers
face in this particular time of enormous publicity and big
money—the danger of placing himself in the service of his con-

tinuing recognition. In that service he is tempted to repeat with greater polish, perhaps, or louder stridency, what he has done before, in which case his trade-mark burns a little deeper into his soul. To the need for recognition, as to the making of books, there is no end. It is finally not enough even to be distinct from others; the time comes when you have to be distinct from yourself, too. That is, it must not be too apparent that you are always writing the same book or play, but on the other hand it is also bad if your work appears to be written by three, four, or six different people. That way you may distinguish yourself as a wonderfully varied writer, but the danger is that you may vary your style out of recognition.

Now this is hardly the time in your lives to be warning you to beware of a mindless pursuit of recognition. In any case, a man who somewhere in his soul does not feel, however shyly, a burning desire to put himself forward, has no business trying to become a writer. I speak on this subject only because of the times in which we live. They are extraordinarily treacherous for a writer. Never was publicity so remorselessly in search of the least signal of a successful author; never was money more plentiful for a successful book or play. The writer motivated by the wish to shine, by that mainly, can very quickly mistake himself for a finished product when in fact he has only begun his rightful and ordained struggle to perfect his art. The pressures of exploitation of literature, the photographic reporter, the television interview, the newspaper and magazine columnists—all these forces tend to press the writer closer to the position of performer. What comes to matter is less his work than the cult which comes to surround his personality.

Obviously, this is hardly the first time or place in history that has sought to celebrate writers, but the quality of celebration has taken on a new tone, not only among us but in a different way in Europe too. The writer, as far as the mass publications and media are concerned, is of interest in much the same way as an actor is, or God save the mark, a politician. He has made himself known and that is all.

Now we have had Hemingway, and Samuel Clemens, and Charles Dickens, and Bernard Shaw, and a long line of writers who were or could easily have been actors had they not been too embarrassed too early in life. Sinclair Lewis actually made the jump and acted in his own plays toward the end of his career, and even so careful a workman and so jealous a man of his own privacy as James Thurber made the eight-thirty curtain night after night in the year or two before he died. Shakespeare was an actor too, but it is important to note that he started as an actor, he did not end as one. I am a pretty good actor myself, despite the impression I may be giving today, and I would probably have become one except that I could never remember lines, and worse yet, have a tendency to change everything I hear. You can't revise with an audience watching, so I act alone in a room, perform all the parts, and come away with the lion's share of the glory.

There is nothing wrong in recognition providing it is not permitted to devaluate, finally, what it is supposed to elevate. Nor is this an entirely esoteric problem. I think it true that fewer American writers have won the mature growth of their art and talent than writers anywhere in the world. As with everyone else, the writer in America is in a country that fits him only when he is young and starting out; as he grows to maturity, or what should be maturity, he is much more likely to have lost his way than to have more securely discovered it. I think one reason for this is the quality of the recognition we give to writers. We recognize him as a success rather than as a writer. It is hard to earn success, but much harder to keep it; evidently it is nearly impossible to forget all about it and keep on calling oneself a writer, but I think it is the only way to earn that much abused title, that much abused recognition— it is, for one thing, to never turn pro. In short, to remain a failure, forever unrecognized in one's heart.

This may sound easy, but it is immeasurably more difficult to really admit failure while still accepting the rewards of success—harder than to believe that those rewards truly have a connection with oneself as a writer. To come directly to the point, of how many writers can it be said that their later work was wiser, deeper, more beautiful than what came earlier? Extraordinarily few. As a class, especially in America, the writer is a great beginner and a very bad finisher.

I do not propose to solve this problem today, but some totally ignored fundamentals of what I can only call the fact of the writer seem to me to need repeating. To start at the end of my thought and work backwards, I believe that so many fine and truly talented writers fail of their promise because they adopt the perspective of their society toward themselves. Before I mention an alternative perspective, let me tell you what I think the American perspective—and gradually the European perspective—is toward the writer.

To begin at the absurd extreme, we cannot believe that a writer who is not known is really a writer. Ergo, the more known he is the more writer he is.

There are various proofs that he is known, which is to say, that he is a writer. He has published a book with his name on it, a play has been produced on the stage. He is more of a writer, however, if he has another attribute—if he has made money with his book or play. He is most writer if he has made a fortune. And this will become truer and truer as time passes because it has dawned on publishers now, just as it did on the patent medicine industry in the 80's of the past century, that the more the product is publicized the more reliable it will come to appear.

The distortions forced upon writers by baths of publicity are not all the same. A Salinger reacts by evidently refusing to see or speak to anyone at all. Other writers are busy speaking to everyone on radio, television, and over expensive restaurant tables. You can be driven mad in many different directions by the same cause.

The worst of this distortion is that it undermines the only recognition worth the name: a recognition that a book or a play or a poem has delivered up a genuine insight into the nature of man and the human condition. That you or I happen to have been the author of it is extremely pleasant, but it is not the point. I try to read a work or see a play as though I did not know who the author was. I try to see and read not in order to lay praise on a person or to blame him, but to receive into myself whatever that work is purporting to say to me. The uses of publicity are such that this kind of seeing and reading has become impossible; in fact it is unimaginable to ninety-nine percent not only of the public but of the critics as well. At the risk of immodesty, warranted I think by the proof it can give, I will say that I try to write in the same mood. To ask of myself, either at the beginning of a work or in the middle, and certainly by the end—what will this add, if anything, to what is known?

Admittedly, this is an old man's question. When I was much younger it would never have occurred to me. I was too eager to find the proof in others' eyes that I in fact was a playwright, and this indeed ought to be so. As I said at the beginning, we must first invent a recognition before it can be recognized, and it matters less what its contribution might be to what has gone before than to what *we* were before we wrote it. But the time does come, or should, I think, when one admits that one has learned one's job and that it is not enough merely to prove it once again. There are and have been writers who have done more through middle and old age and up to the end, and Faulkner is perhaps the most noteworthy, and I say this without being one of his fans. For the most part, however, it seems to me that by far the majority of writers have done and are doing perhaps a little better, perhaps a little worse, what they did before. A writer ought to have the right to shut up when he has nothing he feels he must say; to shut up and still be considered a writer. To consider and still be a writer; to nose about as long as it takes until he can once again enslave himself to some voice that has entered him. I wonder if the destruction of many writers is in part the fear of silence E. M. Forster found; the clarity of aim which can turn back the whorish demand that at all costs he say something, even something not worth the saying, rather than face a deeper suffering, the suffering of silence, a suffering, however, which may honestly open out into wisdom and a new art.

The perspective of society, of the world, is the perspective of competition. Again, this is invaluable for the young who always live in a world of comparisons. It is a way of dying, however, for those no longer young. Hemingway was forever comparing; one year he had "taken on" Dostoevsky; then he was about to "take on" Tolstoy. I strongly doubt that Dostoevsky "took on" any writer, and I know Tolstoy could not have kept such an idea in his head for more than ten minutes. And yet both these men were pursued by a sense of their own failure, but in the correct, if one may use such a word, the proper way. They had failed, as certainly Tolstoy's diaries make clear, and knew they were doomed forever to fail to hear with absolute clarity the voice of their people's suffering. Not the voice of *Time* Magazine, or the voice of the latest fashionable critic, or the voice of the salon, but the only voice whose expression literature was invented for. Which is to say that a writer is a writer not because he is known, and not by how much he is known, but by how truly he hears and sees the essentials of the human situation in his time.

Now it will be objected that there is no contradiction between excellence and the wish to excel, and certainly if proof is needed it is supplied by the competitions among the Greek dramatists at the festival performances of their plays. Nor is King of the Hill a game confined to this age; battles of the books have been fought in many places and in many different times. But there are battles which enliven literature and battles which are nonbattles, such as we have today, in which nothing is at stake, neither a literary viewpoint, a social ideal, or any other question of value but who stands on top of the heap. This was finally institutionalized, as it were, in a long article in the

New York Times Book Review a few months ago. Who, it was asked, will be the new Hemingway and the new Faulkner? Whereupon some ten or so young and middle-aged writers were presented as contenders for the title. The conclusion, as one must expect in the *Times Book Review*, was of course a loud shrug of the shoulders. But even if there could be a conclusion where there cannot be an argument, who should care? And supposing, unbelievable as it sounds, supposing neither Hemingway nor Faulkner twenty years from now, or fifty or ten, turn out to be the best writers of their time? Then truly the crown would not exist at all and the vacuousness of the whole competitive concept would be laughably obvious.

But if the printed consensus and the word-of-mouth augmentation of that opinion is not to guide a young man toward his models and finally toward an evaluation of himself and his work, where can he look? The only answer I know to be unassailable is also unacceptable; it is *nowhere*. Nor am I lamenting this; we live in an age bankrupt of a truly independent public criticism. In one sense it is a fine opportunity, for the new writer today has no critical institution to overthrow. In writing there is no ruling idea to buck or go with, there is no particular style or form either frowned on or overwhelmingly fashionable. The simple truth is that a terribly small number of Americans read books or see plays; I will not even speak of poetry. If fifty thousand copies of a new book are sold it is regarded as a triumph in a country of over a hundred and eighty million. If half a million people see a play it is a monstrous hit and probably a masterpiece, at least that year. So that these readers and playgoers are really tight little islands in a sea of real Americans who don't know they are there and couldn't care less. The pond, as big as it seems, is really quite small, which need not mean that its quality is bad but that the victory it can offer is not the victory it appears to offer. The American people do not play a part in the art works of our time. The working class is all but illiterate, the middle class is mostly sheep frightened of not liking what it should

and liking what it shouldn't. As a consequence, I think, of the
narrowness of the audience, there is no body of peers worthy of
your creative respect. Nobody writing public criticism today
represents anybody, at least not anybody with a real crown to
give you. I don't like bandying about the names of other writers
so I'll use my own work and give you an example.

The Crucible opened in New York in 1954, at the height
of the McCarthy hysteria. It got respectful notices, the kind
that bury you decently. It ran a few months and closed. In
1960, I believe it was, an off-Broadway production of the play
was put on. The same critics reviewed it again, this time with
what are called hit notices, which is to say they were fairly
swept away, the drama was as real to them as it had seemed
cold and undramatic before. Reasons were given for the new
impression; the main one was that the script had been improved.

This rather astonished me, since the scripts were exactly
the same in both productions. Worse yet, the cast of the original was all in all far superior to the second production. The
answer is quite simple; when McCarthy was around the critics,
reflecting the feeling in the audience, were quite simply in
fear of the theme of the play, which was witch hunting. In
1960 they were not afraid of it and they began to look at the
play. It is perfectly natural and not even particularly repre-
hensible. My only point is that had I been a new playwright in
1954, and *The Crucible* my first professional production, and
had I looked outside myself for recognition, I would not have
found it.

But let us not get too romantic; it is all very well to tell
you to look within yourself for your values. The lonely
genius ahead of his time is a hallowed image which probably
infects more writers with monomania than inspiration. The
truth, I think, is that at its best and at its highest, literature
is not the monologue the age has made it out to be but a
personal conversation between a people and its artists. Whether
it be our educational system, our Puritan tradition suspicious

of art, or simply the mechanization of man and his dehuma-
nized nervous system, it cannot be said that a dialogue exists
today between the American people and the American artist,
excepting the kind who decorate packages.

Nor is this news, of course. Everybody knows about the
lonely Melville trudging back and forth to his customs house,
unrecognized by anyone around him, even he the author of
America's great epic. Everybody knows about Hart Crane,
and Sherwood Anderson and God knows how many others
who tried to speak to America and got no answer. Some people
even know about Samuel Clemens trying to hoist some flag
of spirit over an America he saw turning to iron and iron
values. There is one word traditional for the American writer—
alone. Alone as a failure, alone as a success. But what does it
mean? What, you may ask, is the opposite of being alone?
Well, the average answer is, together. Like perhaps a movie
star is together with his fans, or a ball player, or some other
species of entertainer. In other words, the usual response is
some kind of recognition. Like wouldn't it be more cultured if
a good novelist were mobbed in the street instead of somebody
who needs a haircut and plays a guitar? And to be sure, on a
much more austere level, the present administration has sought
now and then to supply a new recognition. A lot of us have
been to the White House. Well then, maybe the solution is
to have us all to the White House every other Wednesday or
something like that. We might even have a National Writers'
Day.

Obviously, recognition of the writer, of his person, is not the
issue. Recognition of writing is. Recognition of what writing
is for, of why it has a mission, of what its mission is, this kind
of recognition is unknown among the people and, for the
most part, among those whose business it is to criticize. What
is that mission?

Now, I am not going to wax poetic about, let's say, the
writer as the conscience of mankind or the voice of the nation's
spirit. No one can set out to be a conscience or a voice for
anyone but himself, and if he succeeds in even that he is

going a long way already. But we are faced with a curious situation; I think it is probably true to say that there are more young writers today than there used to be who have a command of the forms they write in, but are at a loss for something to say. I am sure of this in the theatre, and I judge it to be little different in fiction. From my painter friends I get the same sense of bafflement. There is no longer a battle to establish a new form, at least not west of the Russian border. Certainly on the stage you can now do anything from the point of view of form, anything you can possibly imagine. The shape of realism has been shattered; like all the fixed social ideas of the past our art lies in pieces, and some of them are quite beautiful.

Now part of the work of art is to say something to art; Hemingway's early stylistic discoveries spoke not only to the reader but to all the books that had been written before. Joyce spoke to all of literature, Pound to all of poetry. The speech one can make to art itself has been made.

What has not been made, and can never be completed, is the speech one can make to mankind. It seems to me that possibly because most of America does not hear us we have ceased to try to engage a vast attention and have been backed up into the invisible salon of art. There opinions are made, discoveries are registered, the imprimatur is given or withheld, but it is not the source of something to say. The source is in the way men live. But since the mass of men cannot hear us or will not, how can one address the multitude? There is no answer excepting to say that one can imagine doing it. One can write as though the many were in fact listening. Or, if not actually listening, as though the fate of all were at stake on one's pages even as they do not know and cannot know. For the time being the dialogue can only go on from the artist's side; but it is better than to let it die.

All of which is said in face of a certain number of books which in fact have attempted to carry on that dialogue. The underlying scheme of *Lolita* is a painting of American adolescence as it appears in the middle-aged man; *Catch 22* is a frontal attack on the idiocies not only of modern warfare but of society itself; the work of Saul Bellow has reached out beyond the preoccupation with salable sexuality into the investigation of what man might become, which is what *Henderson the Rain King* is especially about. It would be easy to list twenty books, at least, in the past few years, which are in the tradition of the dialogue with mankind, with his general condition; I am not, in other words, attacking writers. It is simply that if we even had National Writers' Week, and open house at the Kennedys' every Thursday, the other half of the dialogue would not have begun. The people, in short, do not read books, do not answer books, and consequently are not in a position to answer for the truth or validity of books. A National Book Award has about the same importance among us as the Grand Prize for the Best Table Setting. I say this in face of the much greater number of paperbacks sold as compared to former years; I say this, moreover, with no assurance whatever that if everybody read two books a week the country would be a better place in which to live. The Germans, for example, have always read an immense number of books, and the Russians too.

So I am concerned not with the sociology of book reading or publishing, or even with improving the country in this context, but with the weight and the maturity of our literature. To make the statement as unvarnished, as clear as I can, I believe the mission of writing is tragedy. I think that in the works in which man is most human, in addition to being the works that last, and reflect most deeply and most truthfully the situation of man on this earth, tragedy must confront the work itself, the artist himself, and the country itself. I believe at bottom, that the word has not yet entered the blood stream of America because it is a country which as yet has no tragic sense of itself. Without that sense, without that longing, a people does not, strictly speaking, need the answers and the formulations which art was made to give. If a people conceives that death is a kind of accident or, worse yet, an inconvenience to be remedied by insurance policies; if its religion is designed to ameliorate suffering rather than to make it meaningful; if its soul-searching is self-blame and psychoanalysis, it is not yet ready to ask the questions a tragic literature can give.

I am not going to launch into what tragedy is or what I think it is beyond saying that when Christ hung on the cross it was not tragic until He spoke and asked why God had forsaken Him, and having spoken that shattering doubt, nevertheless did not ask to be taken down, nor wish He had His life to live over again, nor express remorse or a resolution to do differently. Above all, He did not say that He felt nothing, that He was not really on the cross, that His faith had vanquished pain, and that He was sure He had done what He was fated to do.

It is not tragic, which is to say it lacks humanity, which is to say it lacks human meaning, when a people presumes to possess the final answer for all mankind as to what life is for and how to live it. It lacks human meaning, equally, when a people, and a literature, seizes only on doubt and will not accept the torture of trying to believe in the midst of doubt. It lacks human meaning if a literature merely exemplifies what dies and what shows the signs of death, quite as meaninglessly although less obviously than when life and what gives life is all that vision can see. The literature I am talking about engages the tension between an event and the human experience of it; between the meaningless particular career and the situation of the race.

The battle of the writer today is not primarily a battle to break through old forms but against a world-wide conspiracy to call things by their wrong names; it is a battle against human presumption whose end will be, for one thing, the destruction of the planet under the banner of saving mankind. I think that so few American writers have matured because only in the tragic confrontation is there the possibility of escaping from the themes and attitudes and controlling visions of adolescence, that time in a writer's life when his usable sources of wonder and originality are richest, newest, and most deeply imbedded in his heart. Our literature, its deepest stamp and line, is the adventure of the young, the young man, the young spirit, the voyage begun, the first arrival. Two authors come to mind, three perhaps, who went beyond: Faulkner, Melville, and O'Neill. But is it not worth noting that Faulkner had to create, literally, a world in which tragedy was possible, a world manifestly his own and not industrial America? And Melville and O'Neill had to cut loose to the sea for an arena of tragic action? Only there, I think, did O'Neill feel at home with his sense of life. Whatever is mawkish, contrived, learned and unworthy in his work comes to the high surface whenever he is on land, where social institutions rule, where Americans really live, and where the landscape is always inhuman.

I shudder at the thought of giving advice to anyone, let alone young writers. To paraphrase an old Army poster, your country needs you, but it doesn't know it. But you have a way around that, you can pretend it does. You can pretend you are not at all alone but in a community, a community of mutes, and you the only one around with the gift of speech. In this dream you alone have the responsibility for proving to your people what they are doing, and perhaps what they ought to do in order to be glorious and true to their nature. Remember, the writer has one gift from life which nothing can take from him—he is describing a species that has to die. So when the mutes signal to you that this world or this country is bound for glory and you are nothing but a pest, you can always ask if that's enough to die with, and if not, is it enough to live with? And if they signal that man is worthless, you, standing at the lip of the grave, you, with time pouring through your fingers, meaningless without your shaping hand, you can reply similarly, that if we are indeed worthless how is it possible that we can know it when the very concept requires a concept of worth. You are writers because you have inherited the ageless tension between despair and faith, the two arms of the tragic cross. The situation never changes; but man does. How and why is what you have to say.

Now, forgive me this delay before your moment of recognition. I have kept you in tension between your own self-doubts and the faith which others may give you in these prizes. Permit me to say that I have won Hopwoods and also lost them, and I know the power that winning gives and the way the soul shakes when, all ears, you hear silence instead of your name. Either way it matters very much and always will, but not as much as knowing that it is not one another we must finally vanquish, but life's brute fist clamped around the reason for our being. To bend back one finger and glimpse what it conceals, and harder yet, to dare remember what one has seen inside that hand—this is the power you have a right to seek and the only recognition worth the work.

AUTOBIOGRAPHY AS NARRATIVE

by Alfred Kazin

Before he died, Ernest Hemingway left a memoir of Paris in the 1920's, *A Moveable Feast,* that is just now published. Anyone who grew up with Hemingway's writing, as I did, and who has always valued his early short stories in particular for the breathtaking clarity and beauty with which he could develop his effects in this miniature and subtle form, cannot help reading Hemingway's memoir with amazement. For line by line and stroke by stroke, in the color of the prose and the shaping of the episodes, Hemingway's autobiography is as beautiful in composition as Hemingway's best stories, it is in subject and tone indistinguishable from much of Hemingway's fiction, and it is full of dialogue as maliciously clever as Hemingway's fiction.

He begins here, as his stories so often do, with the weather, the color of the weather, the tone and weight of the weather in Paris. There was the bad weather that would come in one day when the fall was over—"We would have to shut the windows in the night against the rain and the cold wind would strip the leaves from the trees in the Place Contrescarpe. The leaves lay sodden in the rain and the wind drove the rain against the big green autobus at the terminal and the Café des Amateurs was crowded and the windows misted over from the heat and the smoke inside." Anyone who knows his Hemingway will recognize in these artful repetitions, these simple flat words shaped like the design in a painting by Braque and gray as a Paris street by Utrillo, Hemingway's most familiar touch. And most astonishing, in what is after all presented as a memoir, there are conversations with Gertrude Stein, Ford Madox Ford, Scott Fitzgerald, that are as witty and destructive as those dialogues in *Men Without Women* or *The Sun Also Rises* that Hemingway used, in exactly the same way, to get the better of the other speaker in a dialogue with the hero who in Hemingway's fiction is called Nick Adams or Jake Barnes or Frederic Henry. Ford Madox Ford comes on the young Hemingway quietly sitting in a café, sagely observing life in Paris, but Ford is described as "breathing heavily through a heavy, stained mustache and holding himself as upright as an ambulatory, well clothed, up-ended hogshead." Ford is shown as a heavy, wheezing, distrustful, and confused presence; he scolds waiters for his own mistakes and, as if he were a fat actor playing Colonel Blimp and not the almost over-subtle writer that Ford Madox Ford actually was, he pronounces that "a gentleman will always cut a cad." Hemingway plays it cool. "I took a quick drink of brandy. 'Would he cut a bounder?' I asked. 'It would be impossible for a gentleman to know a bounder.' 'Then you can only cut someone you have known on terms of equality?' I pursued. 'Naturally.' 'How would one ever meet a cad?' 'You might not know it, or the fellow could have become a cad.' 'What is a cad?' I asked. 'Isn't he someone that one has to thrash within an inch of his life?' 'Not necessarily,' Ford said. 'Is Ezra a gentleman?' I asked. 'Of course not,' said Ford. 'He's an American.' "

This is of course standard Hemingway dialogue—it is literary in itself, and it is a burlesque of the pretentious or false civilization that Hemingway always portrayed as the enemy. Yet this artful mixture is presented as autobiography, and it must be taken in some measure as a truthful account of Hemingway's relations with Ford. To suppose—and who can help it —that Hemingway was reshaping the facts many years after the encounter in that café, is to miss the point of what makes Hemingway's book so remarkable a piece of writing. For Hemingway uses the convention of autobiography—real names, dates, places—entirely for his imaginative purpose as a creative artist exactly as a statesman will use autobiography in the interest of his historic reputation. General Eisenhower's memoirs of his first term, *Mandate For Change*, probably contain as many retouchings of the original facts, whatever these may have been (and Eisenhower was probably the last to know), as do Hemingway's. But Eisenhower's intention in writing autobiography is to present a public image of himself for the history books. And while Hemingway's aim is psychologically no doubt the same, Hemingway cannot think of Paris in 1921 without making a picture of the city and a narrative about his friends; Eisenhower, by contrast, stuffs his memoirs with documents of the period in order to persuade the reader that his decisions were made on the basis of the information recorded in these documents. The artfulness of this does not make Eisenhower's autobiography a work of art.

Autobiography, like other literary forms, is what a gifted writer makes of it. There is great autobiography that is also intellectual history, like *The Education of Henry Adams*; great autobiography that is equally theology, like the *Confessions* of St. Augustine; autobiography that is desperately intended for understanding of self, like Rousseau's *Confessions*; autobiography that is actually a program for living, like Thoreau's *Walden*. These are all classics of autobiography, and the stories they tell are among the greatest narratives in world literature. But the kind of autobiography I am discussing here is autobiography as fiction—that is, as narrative which has no purpose other than to tell a story, to create the effect of a story, which above all asks (as the books by St. Augustine, Rousseau, Thoreau, and Henry Adams do not) to be read for its value as narrative. Of course it is ironic to find that some of the greatest narratives in autobiography have actually been written by people like Benjamin Franklin, who thought that he was setting himself up as a model for emulation. James Baldwin, in his powerful book of essays, *Notes Of A Native Son*, writes as if his only aim were to shame the white middle class and to arouse it to the plight of the Negroes. But his book is most felt as autobiography, and succeeds as a kind that only a practiced fiction writer could have created.

There is in fact a kind of autobiography, very characteristic of our period and usually written by novelists or poets, that has no other aim, whatever the writer may think he is doing, than to be enjoyed as narrative. And books like Hemingway's *A Moveable Feast*, Vladimir Nabokov's *Speak, Memory*, Edward Dahlberg's *Because I Was Flesh*, Colette's *My Mother's House* and *The Blue Lantern*, Robert Lowell's *Life Studies*, Denton Welch's *Maiden Voyage*, are so characteristic of the use that an imaginative writer can make of the *appearance* of fact in autobiography that they make us think of how cleverly the imaginative writer exploits "real facts" in novels like *Sons And Lovers*, *A Portrait Of The Artist As A Young Man*, *Ulysses*, *Remembrance Of Things Past*, *Journey To The End Of The Night*, *Goodbye To Berlin*, *Tropic Of Cancer*. Even to mention Henry Miller among such novelists and storytellers is to recognize that there is a kind of narrative in our day which is fiction that uses facts, that deliberately retains the facts behind the story in order to show the imaginative possibilities inherent in fact, and yet which is designed, even when the author does not say so, to make a fable of his life, to tell a story, to create a pattern of incident, to make a dramatic point.

Hemingway begins with the weather; Dahlberg opens the naturalistic poem that he makes of his life by intoning that "Kansas City is a vast inland city, and its marvelous river, the Missouri, heats the senses; the maple, alder, elm and cherry trees with which the town abounds are songs of desire, and only the almonds of ancient Palestine can awaken the hungry pores more deeply." Robert Lowell says that "in 1924 people still lived in cities," Colette in *My Mother's House* invokes her mother's cry, "Where Are The Children?" Edmund Wilson begins his memoir of Talcottville, in upper New York state, with a sentence that more immediately recalls the spirit of fiction in our day than does the flat account of the hero's beginnings in eighteenth-century novels like *Gulliver's Travels* and *Robinson Crusoe*. Here is Wilson—"As I go north for the first time in years, in the slow, the constantly stopping, milk train— which carries passengers only in the back part of the hind car

and has an old stove to heat it in winter—I look out through
the dirt-yellowed double pane and remember how once, as a
child, I used to feel thwarted in summer till I had got the
windows open and there was nothing between me and the
widening pastures, the great boulders, the black and white
cattle, the rivers, stony and thin, the lone elms like feather-
dusters, the high air which sharpens all outlines, makes all
colors so breathtakingly vivid, in the clear light of late afternoon." Robinson Crusoe is more prosaic: "I was born in the
year 1632, in the city of York, of a good family, though not
of that country, my father being a foreigner of Bremen, who
settled first at Hull." Obviously the creation of mood in Wilson's
opening is more in accordance with what we think of as the
concentration of effect essential to fiction, and Defoe's opening
is in the leisurely chronicle style suitable to a time when
novelists wrote masterpieces without being self-conscious artists
in the style of Flaubert. This self-consciousness is by no means
a proof of talent or the style of genius; Defoe and Fielding did
not have to try so hard as Flaubert to create masterpieces, and
they were actually more successful. But art is no longer easy, in
the sense of being comfortable, and autobiography as narrative
is as artful as the contemporary short story or short novel, which
usually obeys canons of poetic form rather than of the realistic
novel. There is a correct and self-limited kind of fiction that
Eliot and Pound have made an esthetic standard in our time,
and the kind of art in autobiography that I am discussing
usually has the tension and manipulated tone that we associate
with such modish fiction as Salinger's stories.

Autobiography as narrative obviously seeks the effect of
fiction, and cannot use basic resources of fiction, like dialogue,
without becoming fiction. Yet if Hemingway had wanted to
write the story of *A Moveable Feast* as fiction he would have
done so; indeed, several incidents and characters in this memoir
were used by him as fiction. And Dahlberg's *Because I Was
Flesh* actually relates as autobiography material that he had
presented in his novels *Bottom Dogs* and *From Flushing To
Calvary*. When a good novelist relates as fact what he has

already used as fiction, it is obvious that he turns to autobiography out of some creative longing that fiction has not satisfied. One can hardly reproach Hemingway, Nabokov, Colette with lacking imagination. On the contrary, it would seem that far from being stuck with their own raw material and lacking the invention to disguise or use it, they have found in the form of autobiography some particular closeness and intensity of effect that they value. The "creative" stamp, the distinguishing imaginative organization of experience, is in autobiography supplied not by intention, but by the felt relation to the life data themselves. The esthetic effect that gifted autobiographers instinctively if not always consciously seek would seem to be the poetry of remembered happenings, the intensity of the individual's strivings, the feel of life in its materiality. Henry James expressed it perfectly when he said in tribute to Whitman's letters to his friend Peter Doyle that "the absolute natural," when the writer is interesting, is "the supreme merit of letters." In Whitman's material, James recognized "the beauty of the natural is, here, the beauty of the particular nature, the man's own overflow in the deadly dry setting, the personal passion, the love of life plucked like a flower in a desert of innocent, unconscious ugliness. . . . A thousand images of patient, homely American life, else undistinguishable, are what its queerness—however startling—happened to express."

Of course, autobiographical writing, even when it assumes the mask of sincerity and pretends to be the absolute truth, can be as fictional as the wildest fantasy. Obviously, autobiography does not appeal to us as readers because it is more true to the facts than is fiction; it is just another way of telling a story, it tells another kind of story, and it uses fact as a strategy. When Nabokov in *Lolita* writes a formal fiction, with made-up incidents and farcical episodes that dip into surrealism, what he is in effect saying to the reader is: This *could* have happened, and my effort is to persuade you, through the concentrated illusion of my fiction, that it is happening. But when Nabokov describes his younger self hunting butterflies in the Crimea, in that other Russia that vanished after 1917, his whole effort is to communicate to the reader the passion and tone of the young man's happiness in nature. That young man alone is the story, and a summer day long ago is all the setting and all the plot. "On a summer morning, in the legendary Russia of my boyhood, my first glance upon awakening was for the chink between the shutters. If it disclosed a watery pallor, one had better not open the shutters at all, and so be spared the sight of a sullen day sitting for its picture in a puddle. From the age of six, everything I felt in connection with a rectangle of framed sunlight was dominated by a single passion. If my first glance of the morning was for the sun, my first thought was for the butterflies it would engender. . . ."

The difference between formal fiction and autobiography-as-narrative is not the difference between invention and truth, between the imaginative and the factual; the imagination is in everything that is well conceived and written. But autobiography is centered on a single person, who may be related to the world of nature more profoundly than he is to other human beings—which is the story of Nabokov's *Speak, Memory,* as it is of Thoreau's *Walden.* Fiction cannot limit itself to one individual's sensations, feelings, and hopes, except for reasons of satire, or as an experiment in surrealism. And it can be shown, I think, that the creative indecisiveness that is so marked in fiction today can be traced to the fact that power is now felt to lie everywhere but in the individual's own judgment. He gets to feeling smaller, more self-conscious, more uncertain of what he thinks and believes; it is then that the novel turns into a document of the thwarted individual will. But this is not a natural subject for the novel, which takes its very energy from the life of society.

Autobiography is properly a history of a self, and it is this concern with a self as a character, as an organism, that makes autobiography the queerly moving, tangible, vibratory kind of narrative that it can be. Everyone knows that the emergence of the self as a central subject in modern thinking and modern art is no proof of individual power or freedom. Shakespeare, of whom we know so little as a person, left a fuller record of the effect of human experience on a single mind than we get from the most tenderly self-cherishing passages in Proust or Nabokov or Hemingway; we know very little about Shakepeare's *self*, and Keats's statement sums up profoundly the creative inferiority of all modern writing that turns on the self as hero when he compares Wordsworth with Shakespeare's bewildering lack of self. Keats says that as distinguished from the Wordsworthian, or "egotistical sublime, which is a thing per se, and stands alone," the "poetical character is not itself—it has no self—It is everything and nothing—It has no character. . . . A poet is the most unpoetical of anything in existence, because he has no Identity—he is continually in for and filling some other body. . . . It is a wretched thing to confess; but it is a very fact, that not one word I ever utter can be taken for granted as an opinion growing out of my identical Nature—how can I, when I have no Nature?"

This is magnificent in its truth about Shakespeare. But it is less true of Keats than it is of Shakespeare, and it does not easily apply to such self-haunted writers of narrative as Proust, Céline, Joyce, Nabokov, and Hemingway. We cannot reflect on such key talents of our time without recognizing the immense role that the self now plays in fiction. The "egotistical sublime," Keats's keen phrase, suggests the sublimity that the ego finds in itself, in its own strivings, as well as the sublimity that it confers upon the world as the object of the self's consciousness. And we all understandably disparage the egotistical, whether sublime or not, especially when we compare it with Shakespeare's ability to enter into so many characters.

But remember that Keats, who understood this lack of egotism in Shakespeare, could not himself write a good play, and that neither could any of the English romantic poets. In our day the contemporary theater, at least in English, does not use poets well, does not depend on poetry for dramatic expression though it may occasionally exploit and impersonate poetic rhythms in its rhetoric. Shakespeare's lack of personal identity is now a mystery, and first-rate dramatic narrative is found only in prose fiction, and prose fiction of the kind, as one can see in Joyce, Faulkner, Lawrence, Hemingway, that has grown out of the egotism of romantic poetry. Faulkner once told an interviewer—"I'm a failed poet. Maybe every novelist wants to write poetry first, finds he can't, and then tries the short story, which is the most demanding form after poetry. And, failing at that, only then does he take up novel writing." Hemingway, whose first book was called *Three Stories And Ten Poems,* learned to write prose in rhythms learned from poetry. From Melville to Joyce and Faulkner, the novelists in English who have come to mean most to us have been those associated with just the kind of self-insisting and self-exploring romanticism that Keats deprecated. And in the most interesting novelists who have come up since the Second World War, like Malcolm Lowry and Saul Bellow, one feels that the egotistical sublime has been their key to the chaos of the contemporary world. Perhaps it is when the world becomes a screen for the self's own discoveries and imaginings, when the self becomes a passage to some mysterious collective truth that waits upon the self to be revealed, that gifted writers turn to autobiography as artistic strategy. And of course the ideal subject for such purposes is childhood—a subject that has become successively more interesting from age to age, and that has never interested any age so much as it does ours.

One reason for this is of course the solicitousness for one's self that is a mark of our culture; but the main literary reason is the belief, which the Romantics first propounded, that knowledge is attached to ourselves as children which later we lose. And it is only when a subject or interest or form is associated with an advance in his creative thinking—which is his power—that it is valued by a writer. No good writer chooses a form for psychological needs alone, since it is not *himself* he is interested in as an artist; he chooses a mask, an imagined self, for the control it gives him over disconnected, sterile, often meaningless facts. There is an artistic shrewdness to the exploitation of autobiographical devices that derives from the fact that since the writer tends to be more engaged with his self than he used to be, he is also more demanding of what the self can make of the world, and that he finds a power in this engagement and demand. There is an imaginative space that every true writer seeks to enlarge by means of his consciousness. The writer seeks to press his consciousness into being—to convert his material openly and dramatically into a new human experience.

The fascination with childhood as a subject in contemporary narrative derives, I think, from the esthetic pleasure that the writer finds in substituting the language of mature consciousness for the unformulated consciousness of the child. Joyce in the beginning of *A Portrait Of The Artist As A Young Man* tries to express the smells, sounds, textures, and pleasures of the cradle. Lawrence in *Sons And Lovers* tries to recreate Oedipal experiences with his mother. Proust, in the "Overture" to *Remembrance Of Things Past*—and this opening section is the classic expression of this use of childhood in modern fiction —describes his earliest impressions in sentences that affect us as if no one before him had ever found the words for these intense experiences. The creative rapture of Proust's own slowly discovering genius becomes the theme of the salvation through art; language can shape and recreate the dead memories that weigh us down, language can raise us from our bondage to self and to the past.

In this power over his past is the writer's key to such immortality as we can ever achieve. Proust's rapture has little to do with psychology itself, for it is not a condition that Proust is writing about but the *recapture* of life and of true meaning. The rapture celebrates the artist's present consciousness, his creative power. In all these great autobiographical narratives of modern literature, from Wordsworth's *Prelude* through Whitman's great songs of himself to the implanting of the romantic consciousness as a metaphor and technique of twentieth-century fiction, the only hero is the writer; the epic he writes is the growth of the writer's mind, his rejoicing in his conscious gift. Of such classic modern books as *A Portrait Of The Artist As A Young Man, Remembrance Of Things Past, Journey To The End Of The Night, Sons And Lovers,* as of *Moby Dick, Walden,* and *Song Of Myself,* one can say that the subject is the triumph of the creative consciousness in the hero. Creativity has indeed become a prime virtue in our culture—and it is this pride in consciousness for itself and of itself that has marked the literature we most admire.

Consciousness, in this literary sense, is not so much consciousness that powerfully dramatizes an object as it is an awareness of oneself being conscious. One sees on every hand today an idea of consciousness that is self-representative. One art critic has admiringly said of action painting that the painter deliberately engages in a struggle with the painting in order to release the fullest possible consciousness in himself, that the painting is the occasion of his self-discovery as an imagination. And perhaps this trait, this growing celebration of one's own powers, can be found among pure scientists as well; Heisenberg has said that to the farthest limits of outer space man carries only the image of himself. The more one studies the mind of contemporary literature, the more one sees what Poe, who fancied himself a universal savant, meant when he said that this is emphatically the thinking age; that it may be doubted whether anyone can properly be said to have thought before. What interests the contemporary critic is usually not literature as a guide to belief, or conduct, or action, but the forms or myths or rituals that he can uncover in works of literature as universally recurring traits of the imagination itself. No one turns now to novels for a key to the society in which we live; we expect that of the sociologists. The only novelists who seem truly creative to us now are those who command the language to interest us; more and more in the last few years the stimulating new novelists have been those, like J. P. Donleavy and William Burroughs, who start from the stream of consciousness and stay inside this world. Such writers protest that the outside world is simply insane, but what they really mean is that it is boring compared with the farce that is played inside the mind. A book like *Naked Lunch* is an experiment in consciousness, like taking drugs.

It is to this pride in consciousness as creativity that I attribute much of the idolatry of art in our time—the idea of art now means more than the concrete works of art. The self is inevitably the prime guest at this party of celebration. And in the high value that we put now on artistic consciousness I see a key to the character of literature in our day. When we look back at Hemingway's *A Moveable Feast,* we can see why Hemingway, for all the radiant and unforgettable pages he created out of his struggles to become an original artist, never became a mature novelist or a novelist of mature life—we can see why fascination with the tone and color of his own growth actually replaced many other interests for him. When we look back at Nabokov's *Speak, Memory,* we can see why this writer, who is so gifted as a fantasist and inventor, nevertheless makes us feel that his is the only active voice in his novels. Nabokov has even written a book on this theme called *The Gift;* whenever I read even his best work, I seem to hear Nabokov saying to the reader—"How talented I am!" Proust is the only writer of his time I can think of who used autobiography to create a classic novel. Proust was a child of the great French literary tradition, deeply rooted in and concerned with French aristocracy, French politics, French manners; Proust wrote his novel out of a profound intellectual faith that the past is not merely recovered but to be redeemed as a key to immortality. The imagination, thought Proust, makes all things immortal in the kingdom of time—and it was this immortality that Proust celebrated, not himself. When the writer affirms that his resources of consciousness alone save him from the abyss of non-being, which is what writers mean when they say that the outside world now is crazy, autobiography reduces the world to ourselves and the form has reached the limit of its usefulness.

Still, autobiography as narrative is usually of intense interest —intensity is indeed its mode, for nothing is more intense to a person than his own experience. This is also its esthetic dilemma, on which contemporary fiction is often hung up; for autobiography deals with a case history, not with plot; with portraits, not with characters; it fixes the relation between the artist and the world, and so fixes our idea of the world instead of representing it to us as a moving, transforming power. It may be that the great social epics of the past are impossible to duplicate today because the plot in such books really hung on an argument about how society functions; today the novelist has no such argument of his own, or is not convinced that such argument is the final truth. But it is also clear that the exploration and celebration of individual consciousness represented an effort to find a new intellectual faith through psychology, and this faith has not been forthcoming. The stream-of-consciousness novel is as outmoded as the old realistic novel of society, for it has become a way of performing and repeating the discoveries that Proust and Joyce made half a century ago.

The story of the artist as a young man has become tiresome, for all such artists tend to be the same. But this is by no means the only story that autobiography has to tell. Sartre said that during the occupation of France, Proust made him think of a lady on a chaise lounge putting one bonbon after another into her mouth. One can easily sympathize with this impatient radical feeling that Proust is not for an age in which we all feel that we are being overrun by politics. Society is no longer a backdrop to anybody's sensitivity. It is ferocious in its claim on our attention, and so complex as at times to seem a bad dream. We have all suffered too much from society, we are now too aware of what it may do to us, to be able to dispose of it as literature. But correspondingly, the new novels of society may come from those who can demonstrate just how much the individual is under fire everywhere in today's world. Autobiography as narrative can serve to create the effect of a world that in the city jungle, in the concentration camps, in the barracks, is the form that we must learn to express even when we have no hope of mastering it. We are all, as Camus showed with such exemplary clarity in his first and best novel, strangers in our present-day world—and as strangers, we have things to say about our experience that no one else can say for us. In a society where so many values have been overturned without our admitting it, where there is an obvious gap between the culture we profess and the dangers among which we really live, the autobiographical mode can be an authentic way of establishing the truth of our experience. The individual is real even when the culture around him is not.

BIOGRAPHICAL NOTES

SAUL BELLOW (1915–) was born in Quebec and grew up in Chicago, like the hero of his *The Adventures of Augie March* (1953), a novel which brought him national attention. A graduate of Northwestern University, he has taught and held fellowships at a number of universities, among them Princeton and the University of Minnesota. His more recent novels include *Henderson the Rain King* (1959) and *Herzog* (1964).

JOHN CIARDI (1916–), poet, educator, lecturer, editor, and translator, saw service in World War II in the Air Corps, taught in a number of American universities, and lectured at the Salzburg Seminar in American Studies. He has won many prizes for his poetry, among them a Hopwood Award (1939). His publications include ten volumes of poetry, several volumes of children's poetry, and translations of Dante's *Inferno* and *Purgatorio*. He is the director of the Bread Loaf Writers Conference and since 1956 has served as poetry editor of *Saturday Review*.

MALCOLM COWLEY (1898–), poet, critic, and editor, has had a varied career which includes service in World War I, graduate study in France, and free-lancing as reviewer and translator. From 1929 to 1944 he was associate editor of *The New Republic*. He has published poetry (*Blue Juniata*, 1929, and *The Dry Season*, 1941), editions of American writers such as Whitman, Hemingway, and Fitzgerald, and critical appraisals of the American literary scene (*Exile's Return*, 1934, and *The Literary Situation*, 1954).

JOHN GASSNER (1903–) is widely known as critic, producer, editor, anthologist, and teacher in the field of the drama. Born in Hungary and brought to the United States as a child, he took two degrees at Columbia University and thereafter centered his interest on the theater. Among his books are *The Theatre in Our Times* (1954), *Form and Idea in the Modern Theatre* (1956), and *Theatre at the Crossroads* (1960). Mr. Gassner is now Sterling Professor of Playwriting and Dramatic Literature at Yale University.

ALFRED KAZIN (1915–) was born in Brooklyn. He has written criticism, literary history, and autobiography, has edited the work of writers as various as Blake, Dreiser, and Emerson, and has been a professor of English in several American colleges and universities. His critical survey of American literature, *On Native Grounds* (1942), established his reputation. He has received Guggenheim and Rockefeller fellowships as well as the award for literature from the National Institute of Arts and Letters in 1949. His most recent book is *Contemporaries* (1962), a collection of critical essays.

ARCHIBALD MACLEISH (1892–), although best known as a poet, has been a lawyer, librarian, government official, and educator. He has published nearly twenty volumes of poetry and drama as well as numerous volumes of prose. In 1932 and again in 1953 he received the Pulitzer prize for poetry. In 1959 his play *JB* also won a Pulitzer prize. He has served as Librarian of Congress (1939–44), Assistant Secretary of State (1944–45), and Boylston Professor of Rhetoric and Oratory at Harvard University (1949–62).

ARTHUR MILLER (1915–), playwright, was born in New York City. After his graduation from The University of Michigan, where he was twice a winner of Hopwood Awards, he returned to New York to write plays, radio drama, and fiction. *All My Sons* (1947) and *Death of a Salesman* (1949) established his reputation. He has received many honors, including the Pulitzer prize for drama for *A View from the Bridge* (1955) and the gold medal for drama from the National Institute of Arts and Letters (1959). Among his other plays are *The Crucible* (1953), *After the Fall* (1963), and *Incident at Vichy* (1964).

HOWARD NEMEROV (1920–), poet, novelist, and teacher, was educated at the Fieldston School in New York and at Harvard University. He served as a pilot in World War II, then turned to the dual career of writing and teaching. Among his books are *The Melodramatists* (1949), *The Salt Garden* (1955), and *Poetry and Fiction* (1963). He has taught at Bennington College since 1948.

PHILIP RAHV (1908–), critic and editor, was born in the Ukraine and came to the United States at the age of fourteen. He began his writing career as a reviewer, then became co-founder and co-editor of *Partisan Review*. He has published *Image and Idea: Fourteen Essays on Literary Themes* (1949) and has edited anthologies of the work of Henry James, Tolstoi, and other American and Russian writers. At present, in addition to his duties as co-editor of *Partisan Review,* he is a member of the faculty of Brandeis University.

THEODORE ROETHKE (1908–63), poet and teacher, was born in Saginaw, Michigan, and took two degrees at The University of Michigan. During his lifetime he received many honors for his poetry, including Guggenheim fellowships in 1945 and 1950, the Pulitzer prize for poetry in 1953, and the Bollingen prize for poetry in 1958. His last volume of poems was *The Far Field* (1964). At the time of his death he was professor of English at the University of Washington.

MARK SCHORER (1908–), critic, biographer, novelist, and teacher, holds degrees from Harvard and the University of Wisconsin and has been honored with Guggenheim and Fulbright fellowships. His publications include the novels *The Hermit Place* (1941) and *The Wars of Love* (1954), a critical study, *William Blake: The Politics of Vision* (1946), and a biography, *Sinclair Lewis: An American Life* (1961). Since 1946 he has been professor of English at the University of California, Berkeley.

STEPHEN SPENDER (1909–), English poet and critic, was born in London and educated at University College Schools and at Oxford. He has published over twenty volumes of poetry, drama, and prose. Among the best known of his works are his early *Poems* (1933), his critical studies, *The Destructive Element* (1936) and *The Creative Element* (1953), and his autobiography, *World Within World* (1951). He has also served as co-editor of two influential English periodicals, *Horizon* and *Encounter*.

For a complete list of Ann Arbor Paperback titles write:
THE UNIVERSITY OF MICHIGAN PRESS / ANN ARBOR